Service Ministry of the Deacon

Reverend Timothy J. Shugrue
Director
Permanent Diaconate Office
Archdiocese of Newark

Bishops' Committee on the Permanent Diaconate
National Conference of Catholic Bishops

In its planning document, as approved by the general membership of the National Conference of Catholic Bishops in November 1986, the Bishops' Committee on the Permanent Diaconate was authorized to prepare a series of monographs as part of a structured catechesis on the permanent diaconate. This second document in the series, *Service Ministry of the Deacon,* was approved by Bishop William S. Skylstad, chairman of the committee, and is authorized for publication by the undersigned.

Monsignor Daniel F. Hoye
General Secretary
NCCB/USCC

June 14, 1988

ISBN 1-55586-240-3

Contents

Foreword

By authoring tnis monograph on the service ministry of the deacon, Father Timothy Shugrue provides a needed service to the Church. He brings to this task his considerable experience as the director of the diaconate for the Archdiocese of Newark and sometime president of the National Association of Permanent Diaconate Directors.

Father Shugrue's critical analysis of the deacon's service ministry provides an honest appraisal of this aspect of the diaconate, its *caritas,* which is very much needed.

Nine years ago the Bishops' Committee on the Liturgy, in collaboration with the Bishops' Committee on the Permanent Diaconate, produced *Study Text VI* which is devoted to the liturgical ministry of the deacon. Since then, there has been some unease in diaconal circles that this document provided too great an emphasis on just one aspect of the deacon's ministry. With the publication of Father Shugrue's monograph a needed balance will have been achieved.

The diaconate in the United States continues to prosper in numbers. We rely on the Spirit to inspire an accompanying growth in the deacon's ministry of charity.

Most Reverend William S. Skylstad
Bishop of Yakima
Chairman
Bishops' Committee on the
Permanent Diaconate

Acknowledgment

The invitation to contribute to this monograph series a study of the service ministry of the deacon offered an extraordinary opportunity for me to reciprocate, in some small measure at least, for all that I have derived from my association with the restored diaconate, and with those responsible for its establishment and growth among us. I want to acknowledge at the outset my debt to three groups of people without whose influence I would not have been led to speculate along the lines of what follows.

The first group is the Diaconate Community of the Archdiocese of Newark, which I have been privileged to serve in various capacities for the past eight years. The deacons and diaconate candidates of the archdiocese, their wives and families, have, by their overall dedication and commitment, their faith and love sparked in me an enthusiasm for participating in the ongoing restoration of the diaconate as a permanent order in the contemporary Church. That participation, in turn, has led to much personal enrichment and, I believe, to my ministerial growth as a priest. In particular, I acknowledge the contribution made by those deacons and their wives and families with whom I have been closely associated in my work as director of the Archdiocesan

Office of the Permanent Diaconate and of its Preparation Program. Here, too, it is necessary to acknowledge the Most Rev. Peter L. Gerety, Archbishop Emeritus of Newark, during whose administration from 1974 to 986 the diaconate was initially integrated into the life of our local Church. Archbishop Gerety's rare gifts of leadership included both the wisdom to be supportive of the new ministry of the restored diaconate and the pastoral and intellectual integrity to encourage careful evaluation and strengthening of the positive fruits of the restoration. To him, and to his successor as Archbishop, the Most Rev. Theodore E. McCarrick, who has displayed an uncommon sensitivity to and appreciation for the ministry of the deacon, I am especially grateful for permission to engage in this monograph project.

The second group to whom I am indebted consists of the members of the National Association of Permanent Diaconate Directors, that community of men and women who are, in large measure, responsible for the visions and dreams, the prototypes and experiments, the reflections and assessments that brought to birth in the dioceses of this country this restored order that has tapped the enthusiasm and good will of so many people. As colleagues and friends, they have challenged, stimulated, affirmed and encouraged me; their call to serve the association as an officer introduced me to new perspectives, new opportunities for dialogue with others concerned with the direction of church ministries. Whatever I have learned about diaconate has been refined and distilled in the processes of our dialogue as diocesan directors.

The third group to whom I express gratitude is the Bishops' Committee on the Permanent Diaconate. Since I was first welcomed into ministry with the permanent diaconate by the committee's former executive director, Msgr. Ernest J. Fiedler, I have come to appreciate the committee's role in contributing to the growth and strengthening of the ministry of deacons. It has been a privilege for me, as an officer of the NAPDD, to work more closely with the committee, under the chairmanship of the Most Rev. John F. Kinney and more recently under the guidance of the Most Rev. William S. Skylstad. In a special way, I am grateful for the encouragement of Deacon Samuel M. Taub who as executive director of the committee until March 1988 was responsible for extending the committee's invitation to undertake this project and was consistently available as a constructive critic throughout its development. That same interest has been shown by Sam's successor, Deacon Constantino J. Ferriola, Jr., to whom has fallen the responsibility of supervising the project's conclusion, and it is likewise deeply appreciated.

It is my hope that this monograph will be a useful contribution to the process of reflection fostered by the Bishops' Committee as it serves the U.S. hierarchy's purpose of establishing the diaconate firmly in our midst. The true test of that firm foundation will be not the numbers of deacons ordained, nor the vigor and strength of the diocesan programs designed to form and assist them, but the clearly diaconal quality of our lives as believers. It is my conviction, better expressed by many others, that we must be a diaconal Church: nourishing that character, affirming and stimulating it, is the special responsibility of those called to be deacons. May our hearts be open to receive the example of those ordained to this office, as well as of those numerous deacons who serve without being ordained, yet whose daily witness contributes to the Church's faithfulness to Christ's Mission.

Timothy J. Shugrue
Newark, New Jersey
June 1988

Introduction

Among the many phenomena suggesting positive growth and vitality in the Catholic Church in the United States since the Second Vatican Council, one of the more intriguing is the response to the Council's restoration of the diaconate as a permanent order of ministry. In the years since 1968, when the Holy See granted the U.S. bishops' petition to reestablish the permanent diaconate, nearly 8,700 men have been ordained to this ministry in American dioceses; more than 8,400 deacons are presently serving the Church in the U.S., with another 1,900 in formation. This astonishing rate of growth has given rise to a series of questions at many levels in the Church, both in the U.S. and abroad. Articulated within individual dioceses where the diaconate has been restored and within the National Conference of Catholic Bishops itself,[1] these questions offer a valuable opportunity for reviewing our collective experience so that the distinctive role of this min-

---

1. See the remarks of Archbishop Daniel E. Pilarczyk and of Joseph Cardinal Bernardin, delivered at the special gathering of U.S. Bishops at St. John's Abbey, Collegeville, Minnesota, June 9-16, 1986, and published in D. Byers, ed., *Vocations and Future Church Leadership* (Washington, D.C.: USCC Office of Publishing and Promotion Services, 1986).

istry can be clarified and its valid expressions can be strengthened.

This monograph is a contribution to the dialogue occasioned by this process of questioning. Specifically, it is intended to complement other attempts to discern the distinctive focuses of diaconal ministry, based largely on our actual experience with instances of effective diaconate. Notable among these attempts has been the effort of the Bishops' Committee on the Liturgy in its *Study Text VI: The Deacon: Minister of Word and Sacrament* (1979), currently under revision. Faced with a relatively sudden proliferation of deacons beyond the traditional seminary context and spurred to respect the roles assigned to deacons in the revised rites of the Roman liturgy, the BCL rightly addressed itself to the matter of integrating deacons' liturgical ministry more consistently into the Church's worship. Because of the visibility that attaches to the various liturgical ministries, it is important that they be properly understood and prepared for. Yet, because of that same visibility and emphasis, it could easily seem that the principle focus of the deacon—in the experience of most American Catholics an entirely new and unfamiliar ministry—is this liturgical role. Deacons themselves have had to acknowledge that their introduction into the consciousness of their fellow believers may often be disproportionately dependent on their liturgical ministry.

Indeed, we face a paradox. One of the most consistent features of the restoration of the diaconate in the U.S., one of its most self-conscious expressions, has been its commitment to promote ministries of charity. Yet, when surveyed, a majority of deacons report that their liturgical ministry and the area defined as ministry of the Word, absorb more of their time, and may even command more of their interest, than had at first been expected. Nonetheless, many deacons whom dioceses might identify as particularly effective will be considered such because of their charitable activities; and those deacons themselves will admit that the ministries of liturgy and the Word contribute less to their overall satisfaction than does their ministry of charity. Indeed, in the estimation of many observers, the truly distinctive identity of the deacon and his most effective contribution to the life of the Church are more integrally tied to that charitable service which the U.S. Bishops in 1984 characterized as "the ministry of love and justice."[2] The attention given to the deacon's liturgical and catechetical ministries, although understandable and even necessary within a carefully construed context, nonetheless has tended to underscore the aspect of diaconal service that should require the least public emphasis (and only balanced encouragement among deacons themselves).

What has been noted is the need, not to contradict the picture drawn, for example, by *Study Text VI,* but to complete it by means of a broader understanding of the deacon's role as a minister of sacraments. In this view, the 'sacraments' of which the deacon is the 'ordinary minister' are not only the formal liturgical rites in which he may preside (baptism, matrimony, holy

---

2. NCCB Committee on the Permanent Diaconate, *Permanent Deacons in the United States: Guidelines on Their Formation and Ministry* (Washington, D.C.: USCC Office of Publishing and Promotion Services, 1984): nos. 35-38; hereafter, *Guidelines.*

communion, etc.), but are those 'signs of service' which he may be able to fashion, in word and gesture, out of his encounters with persons experiencing various physical, emotional, social and spiritual needs. The deacon thus can be seen truly as a minister through whose incarnation of Christian sensitivity and response others can enter into a moment of sacramental encounter with the Lord Jesus. This primary focus of the deacon would then ground his more formal functioning in liturgical rites and would be reflected in his ministry of the Word, even as it would be vitally nourished in turn by his participation in them. Likewise, his charitable ministry would be firmly integrated in the context of a community at worship and attentive to the proclamation of the Word so that the particular sign-dimension of the deacon-as-sacrament would have a ritual framework.

This monograph will examine more closely the 'service ministry' of the deacon, realizing at the outset the limitations imposed by the awkwardness of our terminology (What is ministry? What is service?) and by the still emerging and somewhat provisional nature of our experience. Although it might be said that definitive conclusions should be avoided out of respect for the relative newness of our diaconal experience and what it might yet yield, still it seems fair to take some soundings of our present location and to discuss the results. Course corrections may need to be plotted, even if the general direction of our experience is confirmed. The monograph will achieve its purpose if it stimulates reflections and responses from others regarding the identity of the deacon, in terms of any distinctive ministerial contribution the deacon makes, in relation to other ministers and ministries in the Church. Its method may be more the articulation of questions than the definitive statement of conclusions; yet it will propose examples and suggest perspectives that, it is hoped, may be helpful in providing direction for efforts at recruiting, selecting and training permanent deacons and at providing for their continuing formation and promoting their ministerial effectiveness.

The context of this study is the opportunity presented by the twentieth anniversary of the *motu proprio, Sacrum Diaconatus Ordinem* of Pope Paul VI (1967). It is fitting on such an occasion to examine how diaconate is advancing among us, and what our initial experience may tell us about the trends to be kept in view as the ministry of the deacon begins to mature in our different dioceses and pastoral situations. There are several aspects of our present circumstances that prompt serious evaluation, beyond a mere interest in marking the anniversary of a seminal document. Some of these are statistical, possible now as never before simply because of the accumulation and analysis of data; also, we have passed beyond a point where most of the attention was directed toward the burgeoning number of dioceses in a formational phase of diaconate. Other aspects are more theoretical, reflecting curiosity over the theological premises for the ministry of the deacon and alternately affirming or challenging those premises. There is also the admission of some ambivalence among bishops who, while accepting the generally positive contribution the diaconate has made, are concerned with the rationale for this ministry, in the midst of intense discussion over the interrelationship of ministerial roles and persons, including our understanding of the min-

11

istry of the laity. Finally, there are the essentially ex ternal factors like the parallel (and sometimes competing) developments in 'lay ministry', and the pressure on pastoral placement of deacons in response to the growing shortage in the number of priests available for full-time pastoral ministry. These latter factors, though particularly insistent in some places already, are increasingly part of the picture throughout the Church in the U.S.

All of these aspects lead to a growing convergence of interest around the questions, What is the deacon for? and, What difference does 'deacon' make? While there may be, among those concerned closely with the ongoing restoration of the diaconate, an emerging consensus in response to these questions and others like them, it is naive to think that this common opinion is anywhere near being shared among the U.S. Catholic community at large. As noted earlier, the prevailing image of deacons by which many Catholics in this country would tend to identify the order is related to their liturgical role or their prominence in the ministry of the Word. Again, while these dimensions of the deacon's ministry are integral to his identity, they should not, in the opinion of many serious observers and promoters, become the enduring or dominant hallmarks of that identity. To clarify the perspectives of this monograph, it will be helpful to review the following pastoral and ecclesiological assumptions, consistent with the 1984 guidelines developed by the Bishops' Committee on the Permanent Diaconate (BCPD), and approved as normative by the bishops of the U.S.

Situating the Deacon within the Renewed Notion of "Church"

First among pastoral and ecclestiological assumptions is the understanding of Church, as that community of believers brought to new life in Jesus Christ and charged with continuing his Mission of reconciliation in the world, through worship, proclamation, community life and service. This view of Church applies a fundamental Christological orientation that recognizes the incorporation of the believer into a community which is itself the extension, in space and time, of the Body of Christ. The life of the community, and of each of its members, is derived from the continuing presence of its Lord in power, animating those who have been called and formed into a people whose mission is obedience to the will of God and unity with all the human family. The Church mediates the relationship between Christ and believer, but not as an agent external to the dynamic itself: rather, the Church, in the totality of its manifestations, is the expression of the Risen Lord's call to the holiness and life of God's kingdom, within the real circumstances of a given time and place. It is also the expression of the Spirit-led response of believers to that call. It is, in the power of Jesus Christ, both sign and instrument of his saving presence and activity, an effective sacrament of the Christ who is himself the primordial Sacrament of our encounter with God.[3]

This concept of Church leads to a further consideration of sacrament, as a reality both dynamic (that is, realized in its actual expression, accomplishing therein what it signifies, delivering that which it promises) and relational (meaning it is intelligible within a community of shared understanding and experience). Through such sacramentality, in ever-devolving succession (God-Christ-Church-Sacraments-Christian worship and witness) is embodied the efficacy of God's saving presence, first inviting, and then providing a vehicle for our response to God. This view of sacramentality is broader than, but inclusive of, those specially designated sacraments that the Church celebrates as definitive expressions of Christ's saving action. As an instance of one of these designated sacraments, holy orders, diaconate can be appreciated as a particular expression of Christ's presence, in itself and in its relation to the other ordained ministries of episcopate and presbyterate and to the community of the faithful. It can also be seen as an agent empowered in turn to mediate that presence—to sacramentalize it—in and through those activities and actual relationships whereby the Servant Jesus can be rendered real to the believer, evoking and facilitating one's response in faith. The deacon—not the disembodied generalization of 'the diaconate', but the actual person—becomes the ritual medium whereby Christ is active and effective in a specific way in the lives of believers and in the life of the broader human community. Similarly, the full array of gestures and words

---

3. Ibid., nos. 2-3.

used by the deacon in his everyday interaction with others can be said to participate in this dynamic of sacramental expression.

Responsibility of All the Baptized in Missions

Another assumption holds that all believers are given a responsibility for the work of the Church in its integrated focuses of worship, proclamation, community life and service. This responsibility, shared by all in the Church, is exercised according to specific opportunities and expectations in a variety of interdependent roles.[4] Sometimes the expression can be formal and publicly ritualized; at other times it can be by means of one's ordinary daily activities, expanding the narrower understanding of those responsibilities to embrace the spiritualizing of all daily life. Confusion has frequently arisen, however, over the use of the word 'service'; and, while we might limit our general sense of the term to mean that all believers are given the responsibility to advance the mission of the Church by their participation in activities that promote the Gospel's priorities, we must also acknowledge that in doing so they discharge a simultaneous obligation to serve each other in a process of mutual edification and accountability. The multiple uses of the word 'service' are necessary, at times connoting the general demand for believers to put their time, their energies and their substance at the disposal of those in greater need, and at others meaning

---

4. *Lumen Gentium*, nos. 10-12.

a specific way for some in the community to perform a given function for the benefit of all. In dealing with diaconate, there is the added problem of referring to 'service' as a particular (and, indeed as perhaps the distinctive) focus of the deacon's role; it is this very specific sense that this study hopes to elaborate. Here, it will be sufficient to note that the 'service' rendered by some believers is best understood within the context of the 'service' that is to be expected from all believers' commitment to Christ and his Gospel.[5]

A similar semantic difficulty arises from the frequent and multiform use of the word 'ministry.' But here the conventional application of that term, to denote the activity of the churches' career personnel or formal leaders, actually may be of help in sorting out the points of shared and distinct responsibility in the life of the community. Although efforts to extend the use of the term to describe anyone's personal contribution may proliferate, we will no doubt continue to recognize a sense in which 'the ministry' is a distinctive sphere within the broader context of everyone's responsibility for the mission of the Church. And, given this narrower focus on 'ministry,' it becomes necessary to ask what is meant by it. Is the emphasis on the performance of a certain task for which only some are qualified or authorized? Or can it not include, without denying this 'functional' dimension, a work of symbolic representation within the community? Cannot the ground for valid 'functional' ministry actually be the legitimacy of this symbolic dimension, so that the former is seen as an intense expression of the latter, the relationship of

5. *Guidelines,* no. 27.

the minister to the community at large? The 1984 revised guidelines of the NCCB for the formation and ministry of deacons embrace this type of understanding, saying of the deacon that the essence of his ministry is not *what* he does in terms of sacral functions, but *who* he is as an embodiment of what all believers are called to pursue in a life dedicated to serving others in the manner of Jesus Christ.[6]

The Notion of "Ministry"

What may be said to distinguish the two major senses of 'ministry' is the degree to which the role is entrusted with responsibility for an aspect of the community's life and faithfulness. The more specific notion of 'ministry' seems to assume that it involves more than a subjective expression of Christian faith-in-action. There is an additional dimension whereby the ministry is an expression in the name of, and on behalf of, the community. It also addresses to the community a word or message that affirms fundamental, constitutive elements of that community's identity. It is not a matter of greater authenticity as ministry; rather it is that the ministry of some is to nourish, encourage, challenge and coordinate—indeed, to serve—the ministry that is expected of all. In the Catholic tradition, this distinction, an essential difference that nonetheless does not connote an intrinsic superiority,[7] lies at the heart of the Church's understanding of sacred ordination, which is

6. Ibid., no. 29.
7. *Lumen Gentium,* no. 10.

conferred not for the benefit of the recipient but for the life and good order of the community.

It is presumed that a response to the call to orders embraces a commitment not just to consistent Christian faith and witness, but to the placing of one's life at the service of the believing community, as a means for it to fulfill its mission in the world. Through ordination, one's identity enters into a permanent, as if spousal, relationship with the Church; one is constituted a sacramental sign within that community of faith, an extension in a special way of the Christ who continues to shepherd his people so that they may incarnate his presence in all the circumstances of human endeavor. The ordained minister does not become a mere receptacle of sacral powers or a free lance agent of sanctification; rather one's identity as a living sign of the ongoing presence of Christ is expressed in a collaborative effort with lay believers, in creating the reality of Church that is to touch the world with the vitality and reconciling love of the Risen Lord Jesus. More than a kind of dialogue among different vocations, this relationship is a real communion of lives and witness, evoking from and affirming in each other the distinctive qualities of each one's responsibility.

Reflecting further on the 1984 guidelines' characterization of the diaconate as a "central" gift belonging "to the essence of the church's ministry,"[8] we come to the final set of assumptions about the ministry of the ordained deacon in the life of the Church. If it is to remain faithful and authentic, what does the community of believers need from the ordained diaconate?

---

8. *Guidelines*, no. 16.

How does the community benefit from the ministry of deacons? One interpretation of the guidelines' statement may be that, since deacons have consistently been ordained throughout the history of the Church in both the East and the West from earliest times, diaconate may be termed essential. However, for many centuries, the expressions of ordained diaconate have been hardly more than vestigial, limited largely to a ceremonial presence: in the Roman liturgy, indeed, until the reforms of the Second Vatican Council, priests would routinely substitute in the roles assigned to deacons and even to subdeacons—an echo of some ancient prominence for the deacon, but not really an expression of a living order in its own right. Similarly, the fact that priests have been ordained only after prior ordination as deacons does not constitute a very convincing proof of the diaconate as a vital or essential ministry.

Deacon—Sacramental Sign of Servant

2

If something is essential to the life of the Church, should we not conclude that, with its absence in a real and vital form, "Church" would somehow be lacking an element necessary to its faithfulness and authenticity? Can we then fairly maintain that the vestigial diaconate we have experienced in the Latin Church for centuries has sufficiently embodied this essential element? What, exactly, is so essential about the ministry that the diaconate renders to the Church? Clearly, the limited liturgical functions traditionally proper to the deacon can be entrusted to others (as, for example, priests). Thus, it might seem that liturgy has assigned roles to deacons as an accommodation. More properly, it is a way of acknowledging ritually something else that is more significant about their identity. In liturgy, this identity finds a ritual expression or celebration, based on nothing less than the order's dignity in contributing a distinctive and necessary sign for the benefit of the Church's own identity.

Perhaps one way of describing this 'distinctive and necessary' service is to suggest that diaconate is essential because it embodies or expresses, in the particularly concentrated form of a ritual sign, the image or character of the Church as servant. While that character surely finds expression in a variety of church activities and in the sum of them all, nonetheless there is a specific clarity that flows in particular from the works of charity and compassion, of justice and positive social action that are inspired by Jesus' teaching and example. To be sure, this character should be traceable in every believer's life, but there may indeed be a particular need for a public sign or sacrament that affirms in us the impulse to concerned and compassionate action for others that springs from the virtue of charity sown in our hearts at baptism. Certainly one can say that the Church is not authentically the Church without clear and consistent expressions of charity as a recognizable part of its public witness. Even though at times other dimensions of the Church may seem to dominate that public witness, the expression of charity in Christ's name has never been totally eclipsed in the Church's preoccupation with other elements of its institutional reality. That record is surely cause for humble satisfaction.

The essential character of 'diakonia' derives, fundamentally, from the directive and example of Jesus himself. On the very eve of his ultimate sacrifice, we are told in the Gospel of John, he symbolized his relationship with this world by assuming the role of servant-host at the Last Supper, washing his disciples' feet and so giving them a sign of how they should treat one another.[9] Jesus invests a customary gesture of hospitality with a new meaning, which believers have consistently interpreted as a call to mutual service as an obligation of genuine love. The numerous other ex-

---

9. Cf. John 13:1-15.

amples of sensitive care and compassion that characterize the gospels' portrait of Jesus' ministry have from the beginning of Christianity inspired imitation, not as something incidental to a following of Jesus, but rather as an integral part of the responsibility for continuing his mission. That mission may be described as the incarnation of a selfless love that embraces humanity in the depths of its uncertainty, its pain and its want, communicating almost wordlessly the message that we are beloved children of the one God, brothers and sisters in a common family, sharing in the same promise of an abiding fullness of life.

Recognizing and accepting our personal opportunities for pursuing this 'diakonia' is a constant element of our responsibility as believers: in and through our faithfulness, as much as in its institutional responses to human need, the Church strives to fulfill its commitment, its vocation, to be the extension of Jesus' presence. We all depend on each other's faithfulness; in particular, we depend on the more consistent, more instinctive, more effective responsiveness of some, who manifest a special gift for noticing and attending to the neediness of others. Can we not say that, because God has always blessed the Church with these special persons, therefore 'diakonia' has remained recognizably alive and compelling in our midst? It is perhaps in this way that diaconate—defined as service that not only benefits its immediate recipients but is also instructive and edifying for the believing community—has fulfilled its role as an essential ministry during the long centuries when, at least in the Latin Church, the order of deacons has formally functioned in a truncated or vestigial manner. We must acknowledge, perhaps preeminently, the public witness given the Church by religious congregations of women and of men, that have embraced particular apostolates that embody the corporal and spiritual works of mercy. Notable, too, especially in parish communities, are the many outstanding, if unsung, lay men and women who have bonded persons into a larger context of family; who have responded unselfishly to the demands of Christian neighborliness; who have been prompt to recognize injustice in human affairs and have taken action to correct it. All these believers have made 'diakonia' a living reality in the Church over centuries, and they have numerous counterparts in our own day.

Service—Distinctive Focus of the Deacon's Ministry

But again we must ask: If 'diakonia' has indeed found expression as an essential ingredient in the Church's perennial, if flawed, faithfulness through the efforts of nonordained members, what need is there to restore the order of deacons to permanent status in the Church's hierarchy of ordained ministers? The question suggests a deeper one about the relationship of ordained ministers to the life of the Church. The answer may lie in a reflection on the Church's need to be nourished by signs and to express itself through them. Such ritual signs are not intended to carry the full burden of the Church's actions in support of its mission. Rather, they find their fulfillment in the way they form, encourage and restore the Church's members for their frontline duty of implementing Christ's ministry of redemptive love and service. Thus, our times have demonstrated the need for the Church to establish a means of underscoring not only the manifold needs of individual people and of the whole human family, but also the requirement that service, in love and justice, must be an indispensable component of a serious Catholic Christian life.[10]

It is against this background, perhaps, that the restoration of the permanent diaconate should in large part be seen. Indeed, with the post-Conciliar expansion of opportunities for religious and other laity to fill pastoral, liturgical and teaching roles formerly exercised solely or chiefly by priests, the distinctive character of the deacon's ministerial focus is more clearly seen in its orientation toward charitable service. Because, as an ordained ministry, diaconate is in the nature of a ritual sign, it has an importance beyond that implied by particular sacred functions entrusted to it. It can only be understood as expressing something valuable as a symbol in itself, articulating its meaning through an abiding relationship with the community of faith. And so, distinctive as the orientation toward charitable service may be for the diaconate, the performance of charitable works does not alone comprise the contribution this order makes. The 'service ministry' of the deacon must be evaluated in a broader context: the examination of that context will, it seems clear, determine much about the principles that will guide the selection, formation and pastoral assignment of permanent deacons.

---

10. *Guidelines*, no. 37.

Diakonia—Essential Element in the Life of the Church

3

We have spoken about the importance of ritual signs in the life of the Church; as a ritual sign, ordained ministry has more potential for service to the Church than is suggested simply by the importance or even the necessity of the sacred functions proper to it in its different orders. For example, we would not define 'bishop' solely by reference to sacred functions like ordination, or, in the Latin tradition, confirmation; we would not define 'priest' solely by reference to the power and authority to confect the Eucharist. Nor, then, should we permit our appreciation of 'deacon' to be determined solely by the fact that there would seem to be no parallel function exclusively reserved to that order. Rather, we might propose that, in the Church's glossary of ritual expressions, the ordained deacon is intended to be a word that commands attention, bringing to center-stage visibility the dimension of 'diakonia' with a new concentration or focus, and, indeed, with authority. In the light of this publicity, it is to be hoped that 'diakonia' will be seen not as the laudable response of some to an individual call, but as a constitutive, essential element in the life of each believer.

In addition to calling attention to this dimension of Christian discipleship, the ministry of the ordained deacon is, plainly, 'to order' the various ways in which we respond to this common challenge. The ordained deacon's responsibility is not simply to see for himself the extent of others' needs or to hear for himself the depth of their want, but to help us, the Church, to see through his eyes and to hear through his ears—and to perceive not only the needs of others, but our own resources and opportunities for responding to them. In helping us to appreciate our ability and obligation to respond, the deacon should provide us with examples that encourage us to do so, examples that motivate us to make our particular contributions. He is thus, in the phrase of Pope Paul VI, an animator of Christian service,[11] who, as a brother in faith, guides us to a more penetrating understanding of the range of human needs that lie all around us—often unseen or insufficiently recognized—and to a more effective degree of attentiveness to them.

This may be what constitutes the essence of the ordained deacon's service to the Church. It is expressed by the integration of his efforts in the ministries of love and justice, worship and the Word. In our day this integrated service is lived out in a relationship with his fellow believers that is characterized by a full and obvious sharing in the circumstances of their life. Immersed in the demands and challenges of striking a Christlike stance in the context of the contemporary realities of marriage and family life, secular employment and participation in a pluralistic and secularized society, the ordained deacon today is poised to use this

---

11. Paul VI, *Ad Pascendum* (August 15, 1972), Introduction.

familiarity to communicate a message about the need for authentic Christian service. In each set of circumstances, the deacon serves by providing the nourishment of a sign, an example that speaks of the integration in a Christian's life of the themes of prayer, personal integrity and action on behalf of Jesus' ideals, particularly in terms of a personalized response to others' needs.

Deacon—Reference Point for the Spirit of Service

Paraphrasing the letter to the Hebrews, we might say that no one takes this responsibility on his own initiative.[12] It is the Church which has the duty and right to authorize one who will exercise the special ministry of deacon in its midst. This one then has a particular responsibility, sealed by a mutual permanent commitment between Church and deacon, to look and listen, to reach out and affirm, to create and communicate signs of attention and concern for the needs that he discerns. The deacon fulfills this ministry not in competition with others, much less to their exclusion or as their substitute.[13] Rather, the deacon offers himself as a reference point for the spirit of service that should animate every believer. Obviously, his actions must be appropriate: his fluency in the language of service is proved more by example than by words, so the substance of his acts of service must be consistent with the

---

12. Hebrews 5:4, *Guidelines*, no. 31.
13. *Guidelines*, no. 129.

spirit he proclaims. In this sense, "what the deacon *does*" *is* as important as "who the deacon *is*."[14] Indeed, it is only through what one does that we can most confidently assert who the deacon is, as a living sign of the Servant Christ.

Being "ordained for service" may seem an anemic description of the diaconate, particularly if it suggests that the deacon is little more than a permanent substitute, a minimally qualified stand-in for the priest in certain circumstances. Indeed, such a characterization may at times seem unavoidable, given the centrality of the priest's consecratory role in the offering of the Eucharist and the liturgy's consistent acknowledgment of the deacon's subsidiary function. The designation of extraordinary ministers at times has perpetuated this impression of the deacon as a superfluous or ornamental figure. At its worst, the caricature of the deacon makes him seem a kind of ecclesiastical valet, an attendant to and assistant of the priest in all things. The realities of pastoral life, in often associating deacons with a parochial ministry, carry this identification beyond liturgy. The beginnings of a correction would at least reestablish the primacy of the deacon's relationship to the bishop. It would continue by softening some of the emphasis on a trilevel hierarchy and would focus instead on a tripartite sharing of responsibilities, one exercised in an essentially fraternal association, though marked by a clear dependence on the central authority of the bishop as the keystone of ministerial responsibility.

---

14. Ibid., no. 29.

In the pastoral life of the Church, such a reorientation might help to redeem the diaconate from the perception of its role as adjunct personnel on the parochial staff. For, while the community's access to the symbolism of the deacon may require visibility and some prominence at the parochial level, there is a danger in the tendency to view the deacon as a pastoral associate of above average authority and credentials. It is a danger that threatens to weaken both the diaconate and the emerging varieties of parish-based pastoral ministry. It may be more productive to recognize a 'college of deacons' joined to the bishop and extending his solicitude for the welfare of the local Church in its entirety and positioned at those crossroads where people's spiritual health intersects with their pressing physical, emotional and social needs. Echoing an ancient phrase, the deacons' responsibility would be to to watch and to listen, in order to see and to hear more clearly the dimensions of human need, and to communicate in a sensitive and respectful way—but also with the urgency of an advocate—the substance of Jesus' response; that is his very presence in solidarity with all those who experience the essential neediness of the human condition.

At times, the activity and witness of the deacon in this relationship with the bishop may be more institutional, as one charged with administrative responsibility for a local Church's social service apparatus, or working in conjunction with it, precisely as an employee of the Church. At other times, the deacon may be entrusted with a kind of ombudsmanship or moral stewardship over the charitable and social justice ministries of a diocese or of parish clusters or deaneries with a role, as Pope Paul VI put it,[15] in animating or stimulating and affirming those who pursue those ministries, either professionally or as volunteers. Such a role does not necessarily require administrative responsibility, but would at least include a more personal kind of shepherding. Sometimes the deacon's employment in the secular sphere may be an explicit involvement with social services and community affairs and may provide opportunities for witness despite the nonsectarian character of the agency.

Still, regardless of the deacon's particular circumstances, he can and should be expected always to reflect a concern for the problems that arouse society's conscience and challenge the complacency that so often marks our response. And that concern should be impelled to take action, both in personal witness and in mobilizing the resources of the believing community. Whether or not the deacon is personally entrusted with directing aspects of delivering our institutional response, his identity as an ordained minister, a ritual sign, will usually cast him as a representative of the Church, one from whom a greater degree of sensitivity and insight will be expected. These qualities, in turn, will be anticipated in all his activities, in all the environments that are natural to him.

For example, a deacon—in whatever job-setting, for whatever legitimate employer—would be expected to stand as a witness to fundamental norms of ethics and integrity. Similarly, in his familiarity with the domestic, neighborhood and civic concerns of people, the deacon would be expected to serve, through personal witness,

---

15. *Ad Pascendum,* Introduction.

the positive values critical to each area. The deacon should be forthright in support of the priorities of human rights and the dignity of persons. He should be expected to be a force for harmony and reconciliation in the communities of which he is a part. He should be a conscientious supporter of just solutions in situations where persons are deprived, oppressed or wounded by the cruelties of the human condition. In all this the deacon serves as a spokesman for Jesus' way, as one who can live in the conviction that the kingdom preached by Jesus is not a fuzzy myth to soothe our hurts and sustain our impossible dreams, but a statement of truth to challenge our compromises and transform our expectations.

This description should, indeed, fit every serious Christian believer, and it should motivate in us the same kind of witness and involvement. What, then, is so special about the deacon's claim to this description of his vocation? We may reflect once again that the difference lies not in the concrete results of the deacon's and another believer's faithfulness. Rather, it may be found in the nature of the deacon's response to a call to be a public witness particularly before other believers, and in his ability to maintain, almost in an exaggerated way, his commitment to live as a clear example precisely as a service to his sisters and brothers in faith.

The Service of Example

It is important to reflect on the deacon's role of service in those circumstances not ordinarily described as "ministerial," but which constitute for the contemporary deacon the main arenas where his time and energies are daily engaged.

In his marital relationship, the married permanent deacon serves, with his spouse, as an example of fidelity and of progressive response to the demands of authentic love. That does not mean that their marriage is troublefree, a blissful oddity; rather, the deacon-husband and his wife are challenged to be exemplars as mature adults struggling, in mutual respect and sensitivity, to honor their covenant of union in the daily circumstances of their life in all its uniqueness and unpredictability. In their relationship we should expect to see evidence of total dedication to the ideals of mutual understanding and patience, of forgiveness and encouragement that animate the best Christian marriages. We should notice their efforts to stretch beyond familiar limits of acceptance and tolerance toward true unity of heart and will. There should be an obvious fervor in their continuing fascination for and appreciation of their chosen spouse, the unmistakable proofs of a love that may defy rational explanation. It should be clear that they are joined in a complementarity that is not merely an accommodation to time-tested familiarity with another person, but an ongoing quest in response to the vocation of matrimony. Above all, we should find exemplified in the marital relationship of a deacon and his wife a clear recognition that the exclusivity of the marriage bond does not impose an extreme privatization that makes other people and their needs unwelcome intruders. Rather, this marriage should demonstrate how sensitivity to others and responsiveness to their needs can grow in the fertile ground of an honest and loving spousal relationship and how in turn, the best instincts of husband and wife can be confirmed and enriched.

But while this picture sees husband and wife as equal partners in the enterprise of creating an exemplary marriage, it must at least apply to the deacon-husband, who may, in certain circumstances, be required even to stand alone in faithful witness to the ideals of his marital commitment.

A deacon's parental relationships should also be expected to serve the community of faith as an example of patient discipline and positive encouragement. One cannot expect a deacon's children to conform to a presumed ideal of behavior, but they should be able to expect from him a consistent parental devotion, expressed in above average willingness to listen and understand as much as possible in clear endorsement of healthy and positive norms of behavior. A deacon's son or daughter should have no reason to doubt the authenticity or appropriateness of his love, although it can be anticipated that there will be typical differences of opinion between parent and child over the father's discharge of his responsibilities. The deacon-father's conscientious dedication to his duty as parent must never be perceived as a blind zealotry that isolates father from child, that draws uncrossable lines or speaks in ultimatums rather than in dialogue. To the extent that there may indeed be a fishbowl dimension to a deacon's family life, the burden should fall, not primarily on the child, but on the deacon himself, to create at home an environment that is suffused with the air of Christian respect and sensitivity toward each person, however problem-prone or difficult. One thinks of the example of the father in the familiar parable of the prodigal son:[16] it should be recalled that the father is depicted not only as the victim of a willful son's manipulation, but as the figure who represents God in his incredible generosity and mercy. As Jesus uses the example to teach something about the mercy of God, perhaps his choice of the image can also tell us what he might like to see in an actual parent's behavior. By attempting to live the strength of the father who can love without having to possess—and even without return—perhaps the deacon-parent serves not only his own children, but the cause of Christian parenthood itself, among those who share his call to that precious responsibility.

The domestic environment may provide other opportunities for a deacon's service of example. His lifestyle, for example, has a potential for demonstrating vividly, among those who share his general socioeconomic status, the Beatitudes' praise of the poor in spirit—those who can have and use things like wealth and influence without grasping them close and using them as the criteria of a quality life. In a society marked by conspicuous consumption, the deacon has an opportunity to give a telling example of simplicity, to set a different standard of sufficiency, while accepting the duty of providing prudently for the welfare of his family. It is not a matter of forcing a deacon to prove his authenticity by seeing with how few of this world's goods he can survive. Rather, it is to suggest that the mission of the Church is served by the example of a deacon who, though gainfully employed and fully rooted in the economic realities of his society, still manages

16. Cf. Luke 15:11-32.

to live convincingly the truth that one's possessions do not guarantee him life.[17]

Since it is important to stress that the relationship of clergy to laity is not primarily that of exemplar to imitator, this description of the deacon's potential for service by example might better be termed an affirmation of the daily efforts which believers make to live with integrity in marital and family life.

This same sense of affirmation may be said to characterize the deacon as neighbor, sensitive to the dynamics that affect people in his immediate environment. The deacon should be expected there, too, to be a force for harmony and the building of community. Today, when "neighborhood" seems for many a quaint notion, no more than a warm memory, there is a great need for people to feel a sense of belonging, beyond the narrow limits of an immediate circle of family and friends. The deacon should be animated by an optimism about the possibilities for community, an optimism built on a conviction of people's basic goodness. In the neighborhood, an environment that in America is too often experienced as an arena for competition and comparison of values and traditions, the deacon should sense among physical neighbors the potential for solidarity and friendship; he should sense the vulnerability that so often underlies rivalry. And, in the fabric of relationships the deacon is capable of weaving, people should recognize their basic unity—their common aspirations and disappointments, their joys and sorrows, their anxieties and mutual dependency. Through the

---

17. Cf. Luke 12:13-34.

prism of such recognition, people should begin to experience neighborhood as a nurturing reality—a place inhabited not just by people living in physical proximity, but by sisters and brothers in a larger family.

The Deacon's Service Role as Model

This weaving of relationships is at the root of many expectations we might have of deacons in their effect on larger, more complex communities. In a church perspective, for example, the parish benefits from this service, since in a spiritual context it can be viewed as a model of community. Indeed, the experience of Church—in a parish, in the diocese or as a universal reality—is a sacramental expression of the community God desires among all persons.[18] As such, at each level it should affirm our positive experiences of human community and challenge us always to greater expansiveness and inclusiveness. The deacon is poised to serve as an instrument of this affirming and challenging process, less in the sense of the organizational leadership and coordination that may be characteristic of a pastor, than in the person-by-person caring that seems to be an effective deacon's most reliable trait. Because he *can* notice individuals and respond to them directly, the deacon is also able to notice the personality of a community and the importance of the well-being of the individuals within it.

The deacon's role in the life of the Church community, whether parochial or diocesan, can find focus

18. *Gaudium et Spes,* Chapter II.

in the animation of the community's instincts for charity. First, by helping to create neighbors from former strangers, the deacon can make people aware of each other. He can bring his perception of the need in one to the attention of the resource in another and affirm the mutual service that can result.

Secondly, with his instinct for the potential of each person to make a difference, the deacon will seek to mobilize that power for good, by speaking to it and expecting things from it. While not shrinking from the duty of being a disquieting presence when necessary, the deacon nonetheless typically presses his agenda in a supportive way, gradually leading his fellow believers toward horizons where further needs await attention.

Thirdly, the deacon will often accept the task of organizing and executing initiatives of charity and social outreach. This will be most effective when it is securely rooted in the multifaceted stance described in different ways above. Since the deacon can perceive that the apparent need is an element of a deeper reality, his object is more comprehensive than just the solution for the immediate problem. Thus the technical knowledge and professional skills of a problem-solver are helpful to a deacon, but they will be subordinated to his instinctive conviction that 'being for' is fundamental to any hope of his 'doing for'. In this belief he will be deeply involved in the actual provision of services to the poor, the hungry, the homeless, the sick, etc. He need not necessarily be their administrative or organizational force. His charism may fit him to be more properly the soul of such responses than their director.

It can be helpful to examine this charism, insofar as it can be identified through reflection on the personal qualities—the behaviors, motivators and lifestyle factors—that describe one who can effectively embody "servant," consistently and reliably. Such "servanthood at one's heart" it may be suggested, is essential to a sacramentally effective diaconate, one that is itself regarded as essential to the life of the Church. Therefore, after discussing further the expectations of the deacon's service ministry, we will consider factors that may indeed be primary qualifications for diaconal ministry. For it may not be too much to say that God has issued his call to this order first in the distribution of the needed gifts for this ministry of service. He then invites the Church to recognize in those who are so gifted the ones it should choose to be its special reminders and embodiments of the diaconal nature of our Christian life.

The Expectations of a Deacon's Ministry

Even when the diaconate is viewed as primarily in the nature of a ritual symbol, it is acknowledged that it responds to a variety of simultaneous, interrelated expectations. The minister called "deacon" is expected to be an agent of service, one who is personally and directly involved in satisfying the immediate and real needs of people. The entire range of corporale works of mercy should be integral to a deacon's repertory as a minister of the Church. Such involvement is certainly essential to his credibility as a minister charged with a special responsibility for the consistency and effectiveness of the Church's fidelity to Christ's command of love for the least of our sisters and brothers.[19]

For the deacon, this direct involvement will strengthen and nourish his ministerial roots, grounding whatever pastoral effectiveness he may contribute in other areas. Some clearly defined, practical example of service to another will always be necessary to the validity of the deacon's ministry, and thus to his value for the Church. It should be public and identifiable, without violating either the dignity of the one(s) being served or the humility of simply fulfilling a duty of ordained ministry.

---

19. Cf. Matthew 25:31-46.

By "public" here is meant essentially something done consciously and recognizably in the name of the Church; "identifiable" means something that will be understood to address the body of the faithful by way of example and edification. Ideally, such service should be distinct from a more obviously liturgical or teaching experience (visitation with Communion, e.g., or ordinary catechesis) precisely because it is often our care for the neighbor in physical, emotional or social need that must be stirred into fuller flame. It is our instinct for charity that needs more honing and guidance, our sensitivity and responsiveness to others facing fundamental human problems that needs stretching. The more familiar forms of personal pastoral service in a liturgical or catechetical sense should not divert the deacon from attention to those whose needs are less conventionally accommodated. Indeed, it can be fairly expected that as the more obvious wants of the "near needy" ("our own" sick, aged, hungry, poor, etc.) are increasingly addressed by the conscientiousness of the local believing community, the deacon will look ever farther afield to broaden our understanding of "community" to include those whose right to our attention may have seemed more remote. The deacon thus becomes a monitor of the Church's conscience, calling us through personal witness to respond more expansively to the question put to Jesus, " ' . . . And who is my neighbor?' "[20]

The deacon's faithfulness to his charitable ministry will help to validate his ministries of liturgy and the Word. When he appears as a liturgical minister, as presider or in an assisting role, it should be plain that

20. Luke 10:29.

he brings to the experience of worship those for whom he has been caring, and that he stands as a witness to their claim on our compassion. When he proclaims or expounds the Word, in whatever setting, his ministry must resonate with echoes of the voices of need he has listened to and must yield evidence of his firsthand struggle to speak good news to those who may have begun to lose hope.[21] Thus are the several expressions of the deacon's ministry integrated in a unified witness to the abiding presence of the Servant Christ.

The Deacon as Advocate

Based on his direct involvement as an agent of charity, the deacon can also be expected to serve as an advocate for those who have no public voice or whose demands are expressed in an unfamiliar tongue or culture. The deacon should be an instinctive embodiment of the Christian response to the stranger, whereby love precedes familiarity, recognizing a brother or sister who does not have to earn our respect or concern. As an advocate for all who are in need, the deacon accepts every opportunity to witness on their behalf, directly and indirectly, by correcting misinformation, counteracting prejudice, resisting generalization and caricature of people's problems, noticing who is being avoided or ignored in our thoughts, speech and action. In informal give-and-take and private conversation, in neighborhood and workplace discussions and small talk, in church and civic community debates—the deacon

21. Cf. Isaiah 61:1-3.

should be a reliable, forthright spokesman for those he knows to be in need of a sympathetic and supportive voice. He will also not hesitate to be "prophet," speaking out on behalf of justice and right when situations call for such courageous witness. That he will try to discharge this task without being destructive of his listeners or critics adds a peculiarly Christian and ministerial character to his action.

Another proper expectation is that the deacon should be in himself a resource in support of others' efforts to follow his lead. He should be knowledgeable about available services and materials that can assist persons in need and those who would help them. He should have a curiosity about such resources as are available and wonder about their relative adequacy to meet the perceived needs. He may feel obligated to make suggestions and report inadequacies in an effort to improve service; he should be in touch at least with those church agencies that may have the ability to respond. The virtue in his persistence and passion, however, is matched by the positive and encouraging attitude he tries to express. He is not a short-tempered scold, or a grandstanding critic, but a brother who seeks to prompt more consistent growth in our ability to serve one another from the obligation of mutual love.

Relationship of the Deacon to His Bishop

The integration of his ministerial focuses is mirrored in the interrelated settings in which the deacon is called to minister. Ordained for the service of the diocesan

Church,[22] he is accountable to the bishop in his exercise of the sacred order of diaconate. The community to whom he pledges himself as a public witness of the Servant Christ is thus larger than his immediate circle of believers in a parish or other pastoral unit. His ministry of service is an extension of the bishop's solicitude for the growth and well-being of the entire flock. Yet the deacon is, by virtue of his lifestyle, very much a "local man," tied as is no other ordained minister or any vowed religious, to a particular place and community, by residence, livelihood, family considerations, etc. This rootedness in a local setting may seem to limit the deacon's diocesan character to a merely technical link. But it can perhaps be turned to better advantage if the deacon can be seen as commissioned to serve a diocesan purpose precisely in his local setting. Associated with the bishop, the deacon can be expected to promote a diocesan agenda that would tie the local community more closely to the larger family of the diocesan Church and, through it, to the universal Church.

The deacon can thus be a force for counteracting the negative parochialism that may develop in some local situations. Particularly if the focus of the deacon's ministry is on charity and the service of others' needs, will his service benefit the diocese by expanding the consciousness of community beyond its more familiar boundaries. This view of the deacon's role would require a close relationship between a bishop and his deacons, structured in such a way as to allow regular dialogue about the needs observed in the course of diaconal ministry and about the diocese's response. The

---

22. *Guidelines,* no. 115 ff.

college of deacons, under the bishop's direction, might well serve as an official voice for the conscience of the diocesan Church, reflecting a sensitivity to the Gospel's requirement of love of neighbor that motivates so many believers to expend themselves in countless ordinary and extraordinary acts of charity. The deacons' individual witness might fittingly include such a corporate responsibility to offer particular counsel to the bishop in his supervision of the diocesan Church's ministries of love and justice. Not only would such a role utilize fruitfully the deacons' experience; it would also challenge deacons to pursue their charitable service with greater creativity and consistency, reaching ever beyond the boundaries of the conventional to touch less familiar and more carefully disguised, but still painfully real, areas of human need, whether on the local, diocesan, national or global level. But however it works in practice, the deacon's diocesan identity is understood to confer on him a responsibility for a dimension of Christian life in the whole Church.

The deacon's diocesan character, however, should not be seen chiefly as tying him to an ecclesiastical structure that operates only in parishes, institutions or agencies of a particular diocese. For the contemporary deacon is placed among his brothers and sisters "in the world." It is primarily in the circumstances of his ordinary life, at home and in the neighborhood, at work, at leisure and in community affairs, that the deacon will live out his ministerial relationship with the Christian people, and with the world at large, in a shoulder-to-shoulder familiarity that will be fertile ground for his sacramental witness. His ordination as a deacon is not intended to equip him solely for participation in sacred functions as a kind of counterpoint to the situations of daily life. Rather, it commissions him to sacralize those situations in a particular way, bringing a new measure of ministerial support to the laity in the discharge of their baptismal responsibility for the mission of the Church in the world.[23]

The deacon's status should be well known in these situations and relationships and his fellow-believers should be able to draw strength from his Christian example and understanding from his compassionate attention. However, even if a deacon is not known as a cleric, or if it is of no apparent consequence to neighbors, co-workers, etc., it is hoped that the deacon will still be readily appreciated for a quality of personal integrity and concern for others that is nourished by his ordination commitment. Even here the deacon will be able to serve—both those in his immediate environment, and those who will benefit from his reflection on the human needs he sees and hears. At all times, in whatever circumstances, the deacon is a presence of the Church's ministerial hierarchy with a responsibility to proclaim and give witness to Christ's shepherding of all his flock. Again, the deacon's particular emphasis as an ordained minister should be related to people's need for effective signs of the love and justice that reflect the kingdom preached by Jesus Christ.

The Deacon's Leadership in Service to Christian Ideals

At times, the deacon may be obliged as a minister of the gospel to give explicit leadership in service to

---

23. Ibid., no. 13.

Christian ideals. At other times, the deacon's role may be more to affirm and support the leadership given by others. The specific expectations of the individual deacon in his particular corner of the marketplace will always revolve around his fundamental duty to embody the agenda set forth by the life and ministry of Jesus, especially in its insistence on recognizing the essential source of human dignity, the truth that all persons are God's children. The deacon's task is to serve those who suffer when this truth is violated and to assist his fellow believers and others of good will to discern the consequences of this truth in particular situations.

Whatever the marketplace circumstances may be for a given deacon, he continues to extend the pastoral care of his bishop for all in the society served by the local Church. Not infrequently, it is true, the demands of a deacon's secular employment, or variables in the matter of his residence, will place him technically in another canonical jurisdiction. The deacon should see his personal obligation to give witness to the Servant Christ as owed primarily to his own diocesan Church, but in communion with other local Churches. He will naturally take care to respect the authority of the local bishop in those matters that may touch on his jurisdiction. He will be conscious of being a representative of his own diocese in his impact both on Catholics and on others from different communities and traditions.

Recognition of these two important factors—the deacon's essentially diocesan identity and the nonecclesiastical character of many aspects of his ministerial environment—must, however, acknowledge that as a general rule, the setting in which the ritual integration of the deacon's ministerial focuses is most obvious will be the parish. It is helpful at once to emphasize in this regard the nature of the parish as a community, not just as a canonical structure; the duties of the deacon are directly related to the community's efforts at "love and justice," while linked as well to various parochial programs of a liturgical and catechetical nature.

Relationship of Deacon to Priests

It is important that a deacon be understood as assigned by the bishop to *diaconal* ministry in a parish if the diocesan custom is to assign deacons to a parochial setting. It should be clear that the deacon is assigned by the bishop to a ministry in fraternal association with that of any priests who are appointed to a parish and one that is exercised under the coordinating authority of the pastor, but not as an all-purpose assistant to the pastor or priests. In actual practice, of course, the deacon will render much assistance in the performance of duties or functions which are common to both priests and deacons. But there is a great need to clarify the deacon's role as a servant of the diocesan Church, directly related to the bishop and accountable to him in principle, albeit very often through the bishop's appointed pastor or another priest. Where this three-way relationship of bishop, priest and deacon is blurred, it may seem that the deacon is valued mainly as a surrogate for the priest, simply filling roles previously associated with a priestly minister. On the other hand, it must also be clear that the deacon is neither a freelance ministerial volunteer, nor someone whose job is prescribed in a format like that common among today's "pastoral associates" or other professional lay ministers. Expectations of the deacon's ministry are essentially set by the bishop, ordinarily according to diocesan norms established for deacons specifically. In these expectations, the distinctive nature of the deacon's role in ministry must be recognized as an element in pursuit of the diocesan pastoral plan,[24] particularly as it relates to service of those in various categories of need.

Adequate and appropriate means of mutual communication are indispensable for a fruitful relationship between deacon and priest. "Adequate" would suggest that consideration is given to factors such as frequency and timeliness of communication, its clarity and thoroughness of content, provision of necessary materials and information and the mutual convenience of all parties. "Appropriate" would connote that the focus on diaconal ministry should be shared with common acknowledgment of its specific interest in services of charity and outreach; and that communication should manifest a deeply respectful sense of fraternal unity, marked by an atmosphere of freedom and mutual honesty in dialogue. Deacon and pastor/priests are brothers in service and in relation to the bishop. Bishops need to reinforce this unity whenever possible—not to encourage an identity between diaconate and presbyterate, but to stress their interdependence for accomplishing the Church's mission more effectively. This special relationship between deacons and presbyters should not seem to exclude others, especially religious and lay professional and semiprofessional staff and/or key vol-

---

24. Ibid., no. 49-51.

unteer workers, but it should signal a degree of mutual loyalty that will tend to build up the entire community's respect for both orders of ministry. For these two ranks of ordained ministers share in the bishop's ordinary responsibility for the Body of Christ, recognized not just as the Eucharistic Species, but as the community nourished and formed by that sacrament into a united people, obedient to the Lord's command to love one another.[25] To the extent that good order is required in any dimension of the parish community's life, the responsibility of the pastor for decision-making will be respected by the deacon. Any serious disagreement regarding the relationship between parochial order and the deacon's proper responsibility should not be played out in public, but should be referred to the bishop for resolution, with every effort being expended to preserve an authentic mutual respect between deacon and presbyter.

Within the parish, the deacon may properly be entrusted with responsibility for the formation and development of parishioners for the ministries of love and justice. He need not be the director of specific activities, but it would be appropriate for him to be a moderator or spiritual support-person for those involved in particular projects or programs of service. Clearly, the deacon's role would require careful coordination through the pastor, especially insofar as the allocation of resources may be involved in certain undertakings. At no time can the deacon's relationship to any group of service-oriented parishioners be allowed to degenerate into the development of a power base that would

---

25. Cf. John 15:12.

compromise the pastor's legitimate authority and which would destroy the deacon's special role as a builder of the community and affirmer of gifts for service. Even where a vacuum in proper pastoral leadership may be experienced, it is not the role of the deacon simply to assume such responsibility, in name or in fact, certainly not in virtue of his ordination alone. Nor should presbyters, even with the intended object of promoting recognition of and respect for the deacon, interject him into roles of authority and leadership for which his only apparent qualification is his sharing in the sacrament of holy orders. The deacon's genuine authority pertains more properly to his specific charge to foster the attitude and practice of service. Thus, the deacon will do well to keep in focus his concern for the progressive growth of parishioners' instincts toward the virtues and works of charity and justice.

As noted above, the deacon's participation in the ministries of liturgy and the Word in a parochial setting will be validated by the authenticity and consistency of his ministry of charity. It seems fitting that a deacon should not ordinarily be functioning liturgically or in a ministry of the Word in a parish on a regular basis unless that community also has regular and broad-based access to his witness to charity. What a deacon adds to a liturgical celebration as a representative of a "full and equal order"[26] is, in reality, directly related to the integrity of his link to the celebrating community in his primary focus. True, as an ordained minister, the deacon is called to relate to any community in a diocese without need of introduction or special credentials. The

---

26. *Guidelines,* no. 41-43.

deacon should enjoy the presumption of good standing as a diocesan minister and in courtesy be extended a welcome at any Eucharistic table.[27] But a continuing liturgical or homiletic practice in one particular parish community should have as a prerequisite a dimension of charitable service, well-recognized by that community. This is so that the deacon's ministries of liturgy and the Word can achieve their full potential for nourishing the community, as ritual expressions of that call to service of neighbor which is a constitutive element of the Christian life.[28]

---

27. It is understood that the deacon's liturgical ministry is to be in accord with the proper rubrics and all prescriptions of universal and diocesan liturgical law: neither a deacon nor any other person on a parochial level, including the pastor, is competent to introduce usages other than those established by the proper authority. In the U.S., unless otherwise determined by the local bishop, the appropriate guide to the deacon's liturgical ministry is: NCCB Committee on the Liturgy, *Study Text 6: Deacon: The Minister of Word and Sacrament* (Washington, D.C.: USCC Office of Publishing and Promotion Services). Under revision.

28. *Guidelines*, nos. 28, 43.

Considerations for Selection of Deacon Candidates

Because the deacon, although he has an ancient lineage, is a recent constituent of the Church's permanent ministerial resources, it seems reasonable to assume that the best introduction about diaconate will be provided by our experience with effective deacons. It is possible to correlate popular acceptance of the restored diaconate with the degree to which deacons in a diocese embody a worthy model of diaconal service, i.e., where the deacon's prominence in the high-visibility ministries of liturgy and the Word is balanced by recognition of his consistent activities in the ministry of love and justice.[29] Where the deacon clearly demonstrates servant-

---

29. Although to date the only hard data to support such a correlation have been responses gathered for the 1981 effort by the NCCB Committee on the Permanent Diaconate, *A National Study of the Permanent Diaconate in the United States* (Washington, D.C.: USCC Office of Publishing and Promotion Services, 1981) see especially pages 37, 41 and 49, the common experience of diocesan directors of diaconal ministry strongly affirms that the correlation exists, among Catholics in general and among priests, in particular. The deacon who is active exclusively or predominantly in liturgy or the ministry of the Word is more frequently considered an anomaly, except perhaps in areas where a shortage of priests forces a deacon to assume a disproportionate responsibility for sacramental life and congregational administration.

hood as a living expression of Jesus Christ in the midst of his sisters and brothers in need, the ministry of diaconate is better accepted or received by the Church. Conversely, where the deacon is active exclusively in liturgical and catechetical or homiletic ministries, there can be some ambiguity about the purpose of the diaconate itself. It, then, is more at risk of seeming a way of approximating priesthood while permitting marriage and a secular job.

The diocese ultimately is responsible, then, for determining much about the future of diaconate. Those whom the bishop chooses to ordain, by whatever selection and formation process a diocese employs, will bear the burden of establishing positive and negative precedents that will encourage or inhibit the acceptance of diaconate in the diocesan Church. Those dioceses in the U.S. with over a decade's experience of the restored permanent diaconate can readily attest to the varying degrees of acceptance to date. Many who have worked closely with the restoration admit a growing consensus about the conclusions:

1) not everyone *can* be a deacon, regardless of their good intention and degree of self-discipline;
2) no formation program can make a person into a deacon—rather, a successful process of training and development can only cooperate with some fundamental preexisting traits and dispositions and build upon them.[30]

---

30. Pertinent is the discussion in the book by Rev. Patrick McCaslin and Michael G. Lawler, *Sacrament of Service* (New York: Paulist Press, 1986): pp. 49ff.

Criteria for and Process of Selection of Deacon Candidates

The first requirement for the diocese, then, is to be clear about its expectations of the diaconate in its pastoral life.[31] The second is to bind itself to a standard of criteria that will assure selection of candidates who can meet those expectations. Diaconate—never mind the many things that can be said about it in theory—does not exist anywhere except in and through actual deacons and their ministry. Where deacons are strong exemplars of a truly integrated ministry of love and justice, liturgy and the Word, diaconate earns acceptance and attracts support. The reverse is also true: where actual deacons seem to be only liturgical "extras" or all-purpose substitutes for the priest, diaconate more often fails to establish a clear and respected distinctive identity. Those who are uneasy about applying criteria of selection beyond the most basic considerations of faith and good character may jeopardize the future of the diaconate by condemning it to perpetual vagueness about the order's identity and to mediocrity in living it out.

A commitment to selection is essential to the continued growth and positive development of the diaconate if we are to consolidate the strengths revealed by the initial stages of the restoration[32] and honor the experience of the first generation of permanent deacons. The principles of selection, furthermore, should be de-

---

31. *Guidelines*, no. 49-51.
32. *Guidelines*, no. 65; see also McCaslin and Lawler, pp. 61-63.

termined by the need for a candidate who can be a servant if the expectation of the deacon is that he be a credible witness to the Servant Christ. Determination and the perseverance to hold to a commitment are certainly useful for one who would aspire to be a deacon. But first a candidate must have demonstrated a history of genuine servanthood, indicating the presence of a significant charism for placing oneself helpfully at the disposal of others. A formation program may help a prospective deacon to be more knowledgeable, or skilled, or self-confident in the exercise of his talent. But it cannot reasonably expect to teach a candidate how to *be* a deacon, if being a deacon means more than just the successful discharge of some simple ritual functions.

A selection process should first discern to what extent the talent for ministry as a deacon is present in an applicant. The diocesan formation program must then make a prudent judgment concerning the degree of investment to which it believes it can commit itself in the effort to develop that talent further. This will suggest at least the minimum requirements that an applicant must meet if he is to be considered for candidacy. Only after a reasonable opinion can be formed of the applicant's fundamental talent for the behavior of diaconal servanthood should other criteria be applied. The process then becomes an accumulation of positive indicators: What factors would render the person of apparent talent a desirable candidate for being entrusted with the responsibilities of the diaconate? The question to be answered is always: Why should this person be selected for formation and later presentation for ordination? Never should it be phrased only in the reverse: What would definitely eliminate this person from further consideration?

The Authentic Charism of the Deacon

The deacon, as an ordained minister, exists and functions in a ritual context: that is, the deacon is a sign that communicates a reality primarily in and for the family of believers. Even when his activities are directed beyond this context, e.g., through involvement with nondenominational causes or in service to persons with no church affiliation, the ordained deacon is a presence *of* the Church and *within* the Church. The effect of his activity extends beyond the immediate recipients and contributes to the building-up of the Church in its corporate witness to Christ. The fact of his ordination confers upon the deacon's activity an ecclesial significance, removing it from the realm of private benevolence and rendering it a conveyor of meaning to the Church at large. The question is: How does the deacon's sacramental significance actually operate? One answer would be that it functions in the integration of his activities in the areas of worship, Word and charity ("love and justice"[33]), the conventional triad used to summarize the deacon's role.

---

33. *Guidelines,* no. 35-38; no. 43 further underscores the importance of the integration of the deacon's ministerial activities.

Public awareness of the integration of these activities would seem to be the point of diaconal ordination. If the sacramental power of the deacon is to be understood principally as the ability to produce a certain effect in believers' lives, then it seems clear that this is accomplished most directly when the community has access to the deacon's witness. For the deacon's sacramentality to be most efficacious, it must be obvious that the focuses of Word, liturgy and charity are fully integrated in and through the deacon's activities. His prominence in worship must bring us to a recognition that celebration of our life in Christ leads inevitably to concern for satisfying the physical, emotional, social and spiritual needs of our neighbors, those conditions that contradict the priorities of the kingdom preached by Jesus. Similarly, proclamation of God's Word and reflection upon its meaning, when exercised by a deacon, must be an occasion for aiding the community in identifying how that Word invites specific response in terms of the community's life and opportunities for faithfulness. And it must be seen in the deacon's public witness that his worship and devotion to the Word animate his personal activities on behalf of people in need.

Of equal importance, the deacon's ministries of liturgy and the Word must be clearly grounded in an immediate and observable form of outreach to those in need, however variously they may be described. Thus, the deacon—and the Church to which he is accountable—must be attentive to the community's perception of the integration of these three focuses. The deacon's ministerial effectiveness is compromised when one or another focus is emphasized to the displacement of the others. Yet, it would seem that the least jeopardy is suffered when the chosen concentration is in the area of charity, as long as there is some form of public access to the deacon's witness by way of the ministries of liturgy and Word. The diffidence that marks some deacons' attitude toward public notice should not be permitted to deprive the Church community of its right to see and experience the deacon's ministry. For his "service" is owed to the Church: The "services" rendered to individuals in need are but aspects of the service the deacon offers the Church. It must, of course, be noted that these individuals and causes are not incidental to the deacon's ministry; nor must we think that they are to be exploited in pursuit of some other goal. But the deacon, constituted as a public person in the Church, is now the bearer of a more complex identity: what he does, as a function of who he is, must be permitted to speak its message in the context where it can most fully be understood, i.e., in the believing community of the Church.

Thus there is a need to examine how this sacramental expression can be assured without imposing an artificiality on the deacon's life. For the very nature of his life and lifestyle determine that much of the deacon's witness is rendered outside the conventional loci of the community's life in worship and church activities: namely, in the workplace, the home and the neighborhood. These environments are easily associated with the circumstances of the average church congregation, yet they exist in a broader scheme of human relationships. While in these environments, the deacon's immediate impact may seem to be more akin to that of a "private" Christian in giving witness to the values of

Catholic belief and practice, but even there his effective presence has an ecclesial significance. Even if not immediately observable by his particular church community, his effect on these environments will be evaluated for consistency with his professed ideals and responsibilities as an ordained minister: he will function as a model. And, it seems fairly clear, even within these environments, his ministerial character will likely be recognized as a reflection of some of his distinctive talents.[34]

Some talents seem to be critical factors in understanding the appreciable difference a deacon makes; they help to explain his most consistent effectiveness and account for the fact that even outside the church milieu his "service" is readily recognized and accepted. While the primacy of these talents may be disputed by some with a particular view of the deacon's role, their value seems clear from an examination of effective diaconal witness and, indeed, seems to align well with the original concept of the deacon in the U.S. Catholic community as primarily a minister of charity.[35]

Some of these distinctive talents are behavioral. They include, first, a fundamental gift for listening. The effective deacon[36] seems to understand, almost instinctively, that being an instrument of assistance to another

34. The work of Selection Research, Inc., of Lincoln, Nebraska, commissioned by the National Association of Permanent Diaconate Directors to identify the distinctive talents of the effective permanent deacon, must be acknowledged; see again McCaslin and Lawler, pp. 49ff.

35. *Guidelines,* no. 35-38.

36. Use of the word "deacon" here indicates that the behavioral pattern describes a type of person more than a specific canonical/ministerial role.

requires letting the other set the agenda: The "servant" is, essentially, someone who does what another wants or needs done. When one becomes a servant willingly, another is placed in the foreground of one's attention. The deacon knows that at a certain point help can be offered only in terms of listening: He may not be able to solve another's problem—indeed, some problems cannot be solved—but he can always help, by being present in an inviting, attentive way, freeing the other of the burden of isolation in confronting a problem. If the deacon can ease the situation somewhat, so much the better. But he is able to keep the focus on the person, making the encounter capable of communicating the presence of the Christ whose compassion he represents.

Second, closely tied with the effective deacon's listening talent is his personal flexibility in meeting the needs of others. Being a good servant means knowing when to respond to the urgency of another's need. The instinctive deacon readily makes himself available, even at considerable personal inconvenience. He understands that the incarnational style of Jesus was not so much to give answers or advice as to *be* the answer. Jesus' resources for responding to another's need are contained principally in his very own substance—who he is. So for the deacon and, one would like to believe, so for every disciple of Jesus, the pattern of response is to make oneself the material that is offered up, to be consumed in satisfying another's need. Essential personal involvement cannot be avoided. Thus, beyond a willingness and ability to listen authentically to the other, the effective deacon is poised to respond, to be available, at the cost of his own comfort and immediate needs. Most often it is not a matter of the deacon's waiting for a chance to serve; rather, he advertises his concern in the most convincing way, by anticipating others' needs and letting them know by his presence that they are always free to call upon him.

The third behavioral trait observed in effective deacons is a consciousness of and an appreciation for the gifts of others, a talent that expresses itself in more than just mutual cooperation. The deacon seeks, expects to find and affirms the positive qualities in others, mainly by permitting them to operate and so facilitating their growth. Acceptance of his own limits does not render the deacon insecure, but opens him to recognize how his apparent weakness need not spell failure, if it encourages another to be active and successful for the general good of all. Lest this quality be seen only as an internal psychological mechanism, it should be noted that the effective deacon uses this strength to promote reconciliation and collaboration in a given environment. Through his eyes, others seem able to perceive something deeper in each other. The deacon can serve as a catalyst for the building up of genuine community, frequently by being the bonding element that creates a new and more enduring strength from pieces that previously were scattered.

These behavioral talents, to the extent they are found together, can be said to form a distinctive configuration that describes "deacon" or servant, at least in the model presented by Jesus.[37] But the motivation for being a servant is also important in differentiating the deacon and his kind of service. Imposed servanthood is slavery; and there can be various unhealthy reasons for choosing

---

37. Cf. McCaslin and Lawler, pp. 21-26.

or being content in a servant role. But the deacon is following the Servant Jesus, whose servanthood is a freely chosen response to a vocation, in obedience to God and in solidarity with humanity. Every Christian is called to reflect Jesus' model of servanthood.[38] The deacon's challenge is to highlight this aspect of response to Christ and to provide the encouragement and leadership of example. This example should benefit from the deacon's familiarity with the environments of home and work shared by the majority of the faithful. But it derives its primary integrity from its unambiguous, perhaps exaggerated, embodiment of a model of servanthood expressed in sensitive listening, in personal attentiveness to others' needs and in recognition of the importance of true collaboration.

The motivational factors revealed by effective deacons explain how they follow the lead of the Servant Jesus or why they adopt the behaviors just described. First is the deacon's desire for positive relationships with others; his above-average appetite for relationships of more than superficial warmth fuels the deacon's strategies for establishing a connection with others, characteristically on their terms. Allied to this factor is the deacon's sense of himself as defined by the positive quality of those relationships he considers indispensable. Being known and appreciated as someone who pursues what is good and praiseworthy, who consistently demonstrates integrity in his relationships, is critical to the deacon's self-esteem; it supplies the drive behind an untiring exercise of relational talent. Finally, the deacon articulates his purpose as being to "serve,"

---

38. Cf. John 13:12-16.

"help," "benefit" others. In other words, he sees his own life as meaningful to the extent he has succeeded in making a difference in the actual lives of other persons. Service is not an abstraction or a sentimental attitude for the deacon: It is a primary motivation for the activity he considers most meaningful in his own life.

An ancient formula describes the deacon as the "eyes and ears . . . of the bishop," usually interpreted as referring to the deacon's primary relationship with the bishop and to the diaconal mission of responsibility for those in need.[39] There would seem to be a high degree of validity to this old description, particularly in light of the above, as a way of understanding the service which the deacon renders. The deacon, it seems, should indeed be a person who looks at the same circumstances we all look at, but who sees much more than appears to most: The deacon should be a person who can listen to what we all listen to among the voices and murmurs of humanity, but who hears more—someone who grasps almost intuitively the dimension of need that routinely escapes our all-too-superficial hearing and sight.

The inner resources of the diaconal personality are suited to nourish his behavioral and motivational talents for service. His spirituality seems more concrete and experiential: his prayer responds to a clear perception of the reality of God in daily life, and there is a straightforward expression of his faith in action. The puzzlement reflected in the Letter of James toward those

---

39. See the discussion in James M. Barnett, *The Diaconate: A Full and Equal Order* (New York: Seabury Press, 1981): pp. 58-59, 66.

who can separate their acknowledgment of God from the need to do something about the sorry circumstances of those immediately around them,[40] is commonplace among diaconal type persons. While often admiring a more mystical or more theologically sophisticated spirituality, the effective deacon nonetheless sees a practical response as the most compelling personal priority. Another inner resource is the deacon's physical stamina and level of activity: he is characterized by an energy that seems always to be flowing, but in a purposeful and disciplined manner that is not just physical exertion. He is, therefore, capable of maintaining a variety of time-consuming commitments, over and above the priorities of family and job. And, since in our experience most deacons are men also called to live the sacrament of matrimony, the effective deacon is a person for whom the relationships of spouse and parent are the sources of his deepest satisfaction. Second only to his most fundamental religious beliefs, the deacon's commitment to these relationships is critical to his sense of meaningful living. He understands partnership and mutuality from a well-honed experience as husband and father. More than simply making him familiar with the circumstances of the majority of believers, this quality conditions his ministry at its heart and strengthens its focus not on external functions, but on internal dynamics of relationship.

It is not any of these qualities or talents in isolation that accounts for a deacon's distinctive contribution: but their combination and balanced interplay seem to constitute a firm basis for the kind of difference his

---

40. Cf. James 2:14-16.

ministry can make. They are the equipment for a special ministry of presence that is directed toward action on behalf of others and in immediate relationship with them. They also find expression in and through functions of a more formal ecclesiastical nature, but such limited functions are valuable primarily as a ritual recognition of the ministry of service for which the deacon is gifted, in his instincts, his behavioral strengths and his motivating ideals. Always poised to respond, such a person can effectively incarnate the reality of servant: in such a one, the Church can discern a particularly rich reflection of its Servant Lord.

Considerations for Formation

Once an appropriate assessment of an applicant's talent has been shown to correlate with his history of diaconal-type service, the diocese's formation program can be implemented. The object of the formation program is the shaping, consolidation, refinement or equipping of what has been shown already to exist in the applicant's behavior, temperament and character that makes him a likely candidate for diaconal ordination. The factors that are essential in this process of discernment are the behaviors that relate to the individual's abilities for charitable service. Some aspects of the formation program are properly instructional, communicating information or reviewing prior learning or developing skills for specific ministerial tasks. But it is helpful to repeat that the program cannot so much teach a man how to be a deacon as it can provide an experience that helps him to be more self-confident in the exercise of a ministry for which he has already demonstrated ample ability and background.

The formation program also serves another end: it gives the diocesan authorities sufficient opportunity to become familiar with the prospective deacon in a wide variety of settings and activities so that his presentation for ordination reflects a high degree of confidence in his ability to live faithfully the commitment of orders.

If the distinctive character of the deacon's ministry is the focus on works of charity, then each area of the formation program (spiritual, academic and pastoral) will bear the imprint of this emphasis, and will aim to build up the prospective deacon as a minister of charity from its own particular perspective.[41]

Spiritual Formation

The program of spiritual formation will support the candidate's development as an active minister of love and justice by emphasizing first of all the interrelationship of prayer and action. Examining the baptismal gift of the Holy Spirit, strengthened in confirmation and to be specially renewed in holy orders, the program can build on the experiential bias in the candidate's spirituality to occasion a life-review that should deepen the candidate's awareness of God's purpose and action in his life. This will naturally include a personal study of the individual's gifts for a ministry of service and will look to the ways those gifts have been affirmed and nourished. The pattern of spirituality already evident in the individual's life must be accommodated since it obviously has nurtured and sustained his history of other-oriented activity. The program clearly must affirm what has been working well for the candidate.

The program should stress the benefits of spiritual direction, particularly if that is not already a regular

---

41. *Guidelines,* no. 70-82.

feature of the candidate's spirituality. The program may find it beneficial to share with candidates' spiritual directors its emphasis on the development of the individual's talents for charitable service. A director will be of assistance in helping a candidate reflect on his encounters with Christ in and through his service to those in need.

Another focus of the spiritual development component is the use of Scripture as a resource for prayer, reflection and personal guidance. The emphasis in Scripture on God's attention to the cry of the poor[42] should be a foundation of the deacon's ministry. He must first be able to identify with those dependent on God's mercy and then to appreciate how God works through people to express his presence and concern. The clarity of Scripture's witness in the Old and New Testaments to the will of God that all persons have an inherent dignity and all are part of one family should become a strong support for the deacon's perspective on his duty to God and his obligations to his neighbors, brothers and sisters all. The Word of God is, for the deacon, not a message confined to the biblical books, of course, but those books are normative as the key to a proper hearing and understanding of the living expression of God today. Expecting to hear that message and listening for its clear call in all the circumstances and relationships of the day will be one of the ways the deacon serves as minister of the Word. Mastering the art of listening for that Word is the point of the candidate's prayerful study of Scripture. He should be adept at connecting the Word of God with the cries

---

42. Cf. Psalm 34:7.

of the poor in his own daily experience. His reflection upon Scripture, informed and sophisticated as possible, should always be directed to its power for enlightening the revelation in the present moment.

Because most candidates for the diaconate are married, spiritual formation must also recognize the resource available to the candidate in his participation in the sacrament of matrimony. The grace of the sacrament nourishes fidelity and sacrifice, to be sure, but it does so by opening the partners to mutual sensitivity to the gentle voicing of the needs for understanding, acceptance and signs of support. Such sensitivity is critical to a deacon's ministry as a servant: Embracing Christian marriage in emulation of Christ's pattern of giving himself for his spouse, the Church,[43] surely furthers the deacon's growth as servant. But the deacon will find that the way he and his wife live the sacrament of matrimony will, in itself, be an aspect of the service he renders the community. To the extent that the community can nourish itself on the example of the deacon's own marriage, it should be absorbing the substance of a shared life spent in mutual sacrifice and love. Reflection on sound theological perspectives on Christian marriage in the contemporary world will be important for both the married candidate and his spouse as a way of adding external support to the inner strength of their relationship.[44] It would be especially desirable that deacons and their wives be prepared to be articulate in speaking for the Church's tradition on the sacramentality of marriage.

---

43. Cf. Ephesians 5:21ff.
44. *Guidelines,* no. 93, 106ff.

The spiritual formation of an unmarried candidate, who will be bound to the celibate state upon ordination,[45] will also seek to build on his experiences of intimate human relationship. In his family background, in his patterns of friendship and association with others, the candidate will discern how his instincts for sensitivity to people have been awakened and nurtured. As a context for ministry, celibacy is not meant to be a sterile kind of freedom from marital responsibilities and a resigned sacrifice of its joys. Rather, it must be seen to issue in a freedom for the responsibilities of an availability to others in their relationship with God. A celibacy that seems only to separate the minister from others and from the realities of their life experience will not be a good medium for facilitating the sacramental encounter between humanity and God. The candidate for service as a celibate deacon must come to a fuller, more conscious appreciation of his gifts for a ministry that is essentially relational. He will also seek to strengthen his integration of the habits of prayer and the dimensions of community to sustain his particular apostolate. A spiritual director will be especially careful to help the candidate, and later the deacon, to maintain a distinctively diaconal character about his celibate life while borrowing useful elements from the longer-established traditions of celibate spirituality common among priests and vowed religious.

A candidate's spiritual formation must also build on his familiarity with the dynamics of "the world" and the opportunities for sanctity in the daily environment

---

45. *Code of Canon Law* (Washington, D.C.: Canon Law Society of America, 1983), no.1037; hereafter, CIC.

of the workplace and the secular community. In that context the deacon will be expected to be a consistent witness to the values of the Gospel. Often his responsibility may lead him into confrontation with powers that are antithetical to those values. Yet he should also be expected to affirm the positive aspects of "the world"[46] and to express, in word but especially in deed, a Christian theology of work and of participation in human community and culture as a sign to nourish the believers whose fidelity to Christ is tested in that same environment. Knowledge of the Church's tradition and its relevant formulations of the principles of justice involved in the dynamics and relationships of the world, its economic, political and cultural systems, will be important to the candidate's preparation for his ministry of service. Reference to these dimensions of ministry through the spiritual formation component should aim to strengthen the general moral commitment of the candidate and to further the integration of faith and action in his life.

Academic Formation

The program of academic formation has an enormous potential for strengthening the deacon's service ministry. First, by its basic curriculum and expectations and because of the length and concentration of time and energy devoted to it, the academic component will

---

46. In particular, the Second Vatican Council's Pastoral Constitution *Gaudium et Spes* develops this positive perspective on the world and on humanity's role in its life.

tend to dominate the entire formation process. The perspective on the deacon as a model of the Servant Jesus will need to be kept clear as the academic curriculum and methodology proceed. The multilevel expectations of the deacon in his service to the Church require a broad exposure, though one of sufficient depth and thoroughness, to the full range of theological, scriptural and pastoral studies. Progress in these studies will be an important consideration in advancing a candidate, which makes it all the more critical that principles of selection insist on strength in the basic qualities or talents for effective diaconate. It is too easy for the impression to be given that successful completion of the academic component qualifies one for diaconal ordination. Those responsible for the academic component—planners, faculty and other implementers and staff—must be clear on the nature of the ministry for which the candidates are being prepared and of the fundamental gifts they bring to that ministry.

Although certain aspects of the curriculum may seem to have limited immediate practical value for a deacon, nonetheless the candidate should see them related to his posture as a servant of the Church, at least in the sense of being a public representative of the Church, and therefore likely to be of greater service to people by reason of his knowledge and general information about it. However, there must be serious attention given to developing a particular curriculum for diaconal ministry, one that is specific to the real needs of deacons, and neither a compressed seminary course nor an upgraded adult education program. Perhaps inevitably, much of the curriculum will be derived from seminary models of education, and there is an advantage to making diaconate training programs more inclusive of those aspiring to other ministerial roles as laity. The issue of a sensible curriculum for diaconate, though, is the real point: Care must be taken to counter the view that, because of the training model, the deacon is "not quite" the equivalent of a priest or other seminary graduate or lay professional, but "a little more" than a lay volunteer in ministry. The relationships among ministers, furthermore, must not be determined solely on the basis of the perceived weight or prestige of their respective training backgrounds. Competency must be demanded of all; adequacy of preparation must be expected of all and by all. But adequacy should be related more to the question of appropriateness for one's intended ministry than to an artificial system that would stratify different "classes" of ministers.

Much of the pressure on the academic component to produce deacons, however, can be relieved by applying sensible criteria of selection. A candidate strong in fundamental diaconal qualities and behavior will recognize the academic program's potential for enhancing his ministerial usefulness. He will perceive that his object is not to study "how to be a deacon," but to familiarize himself with the various aspects of the Church's self-understanding and tradition and with relevant pastoral information and insights so that his service to those in need will be that of an authoritative representative of the Church. However the academic curriculum is designed to meet the prescribed expectations of the bishops' guidelines,[47] it will be helpful if its objective is clearly to assist the candidate in a mature

47. *Guidelines,* no. 75-81.

review of his understanding of essential Catholic doctrine and practice in light of his adult experience. The candidate should be encouraged to pose the religious questions he has himself formulated as well as those he has heard among his peers. Similarly, he should be prompted to recognize and respect challenges to a simplistic understanding of the Catholic tradition whether originating in his own mind, among others of his acquaintance, from our culture or even from sources hostile to religion. A heightened sensitivity to the genuinely religious aspects of people's questions will make the deacon a good minister for the Church's sake as he promotes a dialogue that seeks to share effectively the Church's witness to the message of Jesus Christ. His acknowledgment of the legitimacy of a questioning process will render him a helpful servant of others who may welcome the example of one who is quietly confident in his faith but not judgmental or condescending when confronted with another's hesitancy or doubts. Moreover, the deacon will most often be in circumstances where his theological fluency and sophistication will be less pointedly tested than the unqualified consistency of his Christian charity. This is not to put learning and practice in mutually opposing positions; it is simply to note the importance of insuring that the deacon has absorbed in its fullness the spirit of Christian love that precedes and animates the Church's doctrinal reflections. The deacon will likely be successful less because of his ability—valuable though it will be— to talk convincingly about God's love, than because of his talent for enveloping others in the reality of a love which then bespeaks his intimate knowledge of the God of compassion.

Further, it will be necessary for the academic curriculum to deepen candidates' familiarity with Scripture's witness to this compassionate God, and with the doctrinal and ethical norms that derive from the Church's meditation on it. This will be important not just for the candidates' own spiritual growth, but also for their role as ministers of the Word, with a particular ear for its emphasis on the imperative of love for all who are created in God's image and likeness. Indeed, the deacon will respect his ministry as an expression of the Incarnation of that Word in Jesus Christ, and will value his familiarity with Scripture as an indispensable means of remaining in communion with Jesus. At the same time, the candidate's training in Scripture should prepare him for a competent and confident exercise of all the liturgical and homiletic ministries of the Word that are proper to a deacon.[48]

Pastoral Formation

The 1984 guidelines of the U.S. Bishops make it clear that the entire training program for diaconal candidates should be cast in terms of its pastoral usefulness.[49] Beyond a foundational review of Catholic doctrine and a thorough preparation for lifelong study of Scripture, the curriculum must also cover the areas of liturgy and sacraments, Church history, moral theology and canon law to a degree sufficient to prepare the candidate to

---

48. Ibid., no. 39-40; cf. also *Study Text 6: The Deacon: Minister of Word and Sacrament.*

49. *Guidelines,* no. 82.

be a knowledgeable representative of the Church and a proficient minister of its rites. It will also review data drawn from the fields of psychology and sociology that will permit a more informed application of basic principles of pastoral care.

More specifically, the training curriculum will include opportunities for the development of a candidate's personal skills in pastoral practice. These opportunities will be based on a presentation of the fundamentals of pastoral counseling, stressing particularly the limits to be observed in situations requiring special expertise and professional intervention.[50] The program would do well to address itself to the preexisting talent and disposition of the candidate to listen attentively to others. Practical advice to improve listening skills will be productive in many areas of a deacon's ministry, since he usually has an instinct about listening as an indispensable prerequisite for effective interpersonal ministry. The prudent diocesan training program will be modest in its expectations of being able to qualify all deacons as professionals or even paraprofessionals in counseling. But it will also recognize the deacon's contribution as a listening presence of uncommon sensitivity and it will seek not just to clarify the limits of a deacon's qualifications, but also to equip each deacon to make intelligent referrals to appropriate resources. Naturally, a deacon who antic-

---

50. There is a growing interest in establishing clear diocesan guidelines for a deacon's exercise of any counseling role as a cleric, particularly in view of the legal opinions on "agency" as it applies to a deacon and on the liability the Church may incur as a consequence of his incardination in a given diocese.

ipates an assignment obliging him to be more directly responsible for a counseling ministry will need to be properly trained and authorized. Simply being accorded the status of an ordained minister does not qualify one for the complex demands of serious counseling situations. The caution here is directed toward the giving of advice or prescribing of solutions in situations more sensitive than the routine pastoral variety. The deacon should not underestimate the weight others may attach to a casual comment uttered by a cleric. The deacon can always be a sympathetic listener, with an obligation both to a proper confidentiality[51] and to referral to more qualified resource-persons. Referral does not mean refusal to help. At the very least, the Church would expect the deacon to be the good listener in the first instance and one who can make appropriate referrals or know whom to consult before offering advice.

Usually, the circumstances of a candidate's formation will incorporate ongoing involvement in actual service situations. Based on the diocesan pastoral plan's expectations of deacons' ministry[52] and considering the particular requirements of the pastoral unit that may be sponsoring an individual's candidacy, these situations may take a variety of forms. The purpose of the candidate's involvement is threefold: first, to broaden his experience and strengthen his confidence in meeting different ministerial demands; secondly, to assist in the

---

51. A deacon should know when the ordinary expectation of confidentiality may be qualified by applicable law or other considerations. Dioceses need to develop policies that will clearly define the protections that may extend to deacons as well as the limits they must observe.

52. *Guidelines*, no. 50.

actual meeting of the needs; and thirdly, to provide the formation program with further opportunities to observe the candidate's diaconal behavior and instincts. All these factors will influence the pattern of involvement that is either chosen by a candidate or prescribed for him by the formation program.

Since this service activity is seen as an integral part of a candidate's formation, it will be most helpful if the situation is viewed primarily as a learning experience. It will then aim to provide background information, skill development and material for theological and pastoral reflection. It may take the highly structured form of clinical pastoral education or be implemented along less formal lines. In any case, appropriate supervision will be important if the experience is to offer a candidate the greatest benefit. The candidate should be able to perceive the objectives of each phase of this service activity as they involve particular areas of theory and skill and as they relate to an affirmation of his fundamental instincts for diaconal ministry. These objectives should also be made clear to all instructional and/or supervisory personnel. Ultimately it is the formation program itself that must assume responsibility for assessing what the candidate learns from his experiences and how well he is able to perform in his various service activities.

A formation program may find it useful to propose a system of required and elective units that will meet both the diocese's need for a common base of experiences and the candidate's need for variety and preference in the discovery and exercise of individual talent and aptitude. Units should be of sufficient duration to permit more than a casual acquaintance with an area of service and should blend theory or analysis with actual practice. In the practice experiences, attention should be given to how the candidate's primary diaconal talents—his ability to listen to another, to involve others and encourage them in their ministry and to bend to meet their needs—have been engaged and confirmed. More general areas (e.g., pastoral care of the sick in hospitals or at home; nursing home ministry; soup kitchen and shelter work; ministry with the disabled, etc.) may comprise the units required of all candidates. More particularized areas requiring special preparation and personal preference (e.g., prison ministry; bereavement counseling; hospice work with the terminally ill; ministry with troubled youth, with persons suffering various addictions, with the separated and divorced, etc.) may be left to the choice of the candidate. At some point in the formation process, it would be desirable for the candidate to develop a ministry initiative that demonstrates his grasp of his own talents and of the actual needs that demand attention in a given setting. The formation program can assist in identifying resource people whose related experience may enable them to help the candidate learn more effectively.

Evaluation of the Deacon Candidate

The process of evaluating how these general and specific experiences have helped the candidate to be a more effective minister should include his own reflections, the observations of designated supervisors and the opinions of those who have been served in the particular ministry setting. The formation program will have to determine how these differing reports are integrated to offer a fair estimate of the candidate's successful performance. The precise aspects to be looked for from each of these evaluators will need to be clearly spelled out: i.e., both the candidate and those evaluating him will have to share certain realistic expectations about the outcomes of these experiences. It would be most helpful for the formation program to designate a staff membeer or identify some other person who could function as a mentor for the candidate, meeting regularly with him to review his service experiences and facilitate his reflection on what may have been learned. Such a mentor should avoid too quick an intervention with a narrative of his or her own learning experiences, but should be able to use that experience as a guide to pose appropriate questions for the candidate's consideration.

The focus of the candidate's self-evaluation and that of any supervisor, mentor or other observer should be on the effectiveness of a particular behavior as a sacramental sign as well as on the appropriateness of any helping action in itself and the expertise with which it is offered. The "professionalism" of the deacon as a minister cannot be measured adequately if only the skill and correctness of his ministerial behavior is considered. Rather, his behavior must also be seen in context as an expression of an incarnational reality through which a person encounters God in the particular circumstances in which the deacon represents the Servant Jesus. In this properly sacramental experience, the dimensions of word and action should be so integrated that in the instance of a given service being rendered, the reality of God's love is discovered. The ministerial skill or artistry of the deacon will be more authentically perceived in the manner in which he is able to fashion a moment that speaks of God compellingly, with unambiguous but almost wordless clarity, more by actions congruent with the gospel descriptions of Jesus than by a verbal commentary.

As an embodiment of the sacrament of orders, the deacon should thus be encountered in the graceful unity of what he says and does as an authoritative contact with Jesus, the Incarnation of God's love, the Word spoken in the language of service, vulnerable to all the needs of the human family. As a minister of the Eucharist, the deacon is responsible especially for creating parallel illustrations in obedience to Jesus' command, " ' . . . do this in memory of me,' "[53] really laying down his life, putting himself at the disposal of the Lord who extends his reassuring hand to touch the whole world of human need.

Such sacramental authenticity necessarily includes skill, competence and sensitivity in the performance of ministerial and human services, but it is not fully achieved simply by the sum of these elements. The inner spirit that should animate true ministry must be discernible, underlying and penetrating the given behavior that seeks to bring relief to a brother or sister in need. The mission of the servant of Yahweh,[54] resonant in the life and ministry of Jesus, must be recognized in the deacon as well, revealing the action of a God who would deliver his people from every infirmity and every

---

53. Luke 22:19.
54. Cf. Isaiah 61:1-3; Luke 4:16-22.

form of bondage. It is this revelatory significance that separates the deacon's ministry from a kind of philanthropy or altruistic do-goodism and renders it a source of grace for the believing community. It is the deacon's obligation to work to combine the practical skills necessary for helpful and competent service with a transparent selflessness that will communicate nothing so clearly as the truth that God is love. A consistent testimony to the candidate's ability to imaging and articulating this truth in action should be the real object sought in evaluations of his performance in the various service units of the formation process.

Without evidence of this ability, the Church is insufficiently informed to voice its confidence in the candidate as an authoritative witness to the continuing ministry of the Servant Christ. Through ordination and the granting of canonical faculties, the local diocesan Church establishes the deacon as its minister. Indeed, receiving the faculties for ministry is for the deacon not so much the obtaining of permission to perform some activity heretofore impossible—after all, much of a deacon's time will be spent in activities in which he has long been involved or in which others freely participate—rather, it is the authorization to represent the Church in an intensively personal way: to be, in himself, an assured locus of the encounter between God and his people. For this authorization to be most meaningful, the Church must have seen in the candidate for ordination clear evidence of his ability to integrate, in formal ministerial functions and in the daily circumstances of his life in "the world," the emphases on charity (love and justice), worship (in spirit and truth) and Word (made flesh).

The several components of the formation or training process find integration as they contribute to the discovery and support of this ability. His vocation to the ministry of the diaconate being affirmed in this process, the candidate is thereby strengthened to respond when the Church voices God's invitation in the call to orders. Stepping forward for the laying-on of hands, the candidate kneels as a believer with diaconal instincts and a reliable spirit of selflessness. He rises a sacramental presence, a minister with a responsibility to nourish, affirm and challenge those instincts and that spirit in others, through the signs he fashions from his encounters with brothers and sisters in all kinds of need. The Church's prayer is that the God "who began the good work"[55] in the deacon will bring it to completion in and through a lifelong ministry of faithful witness.

---

55. *Rite of Ordination of a Deacon,* no. 16.

Considerations for
Deacon Placement

The typical Catholic deacon in the U.S. exercises a ministry that is difficult to describe in simple terms. Most often remaining responsible for his own livelihood and that of his family from non-Church employment, the deacon is usually not available for full-time duty in a manner similar to the norm for priests, religious and, increasingly, for lay ministry professionals. Yet, the deacon's ordination most definitely establishes him as a full-time sacramental presence, responsible as a minister twenty-four hours a day for serving the life of the church community. The fact that this presence is felt most of the time in settings familiarly, if somewhat inaccurately, known as 'the marketplace'—in the environments of home and family, neighborhood and secular community and workplace—makes it important for the diocesan Church to be clear about the deacon's ministerial presence and how it affects pastoral life. For it is the diocesan Church which calls the deacon to accountability, providing the context in which the deacon's ministry complements that of others, while making its particular contribution to the building-up of the kingdom.

It is essential, first of all, to acknowledge that although the settings for so much of the deacon's activity are not in conventional *ecclesiastical* structures or institutes, nonetheless there is an enormous *ecclesial* significance to what he does and who he is in those settings. Immersed in the circumstances that absorb so much energy and occupy such importance in the daily life of most believers, the deacon there has conceivably his greatest impact on the Church's life. There he stands shoulder-to-shoulder with those who, according to Vatican II[56] have responsibility for bringing the Gospel to bear on the realities of secular life. If it is properly the vocation of the laity to be the principal agents of the Church's mission in "the world," then all the circumstances of secular reality comprise the arena of ecclesial activity. The deacon, then, lives his theological relationship with the *ecclesia,* day in and day out, according to dynamics recognizably different from those that govern the relationship between the community and the majority of priests, religious and lay ministry professionals.

A description of this relationship between the deacon and his fellow believers was attempted elsewhere.[57] How effective this relationship is in actuality depends on a variety of factors: Is the deacon known explicitly as such among the people he encounters, particularly his fellow-believers? Does his identity make a difference in the way he interacts with them, whether from his point of view or theirs? Is there an observable connection between his witness and the fundamental imperative for all believers to imitate the charity of Christ? Is his

---

56. *Decree on the Apostolate of Lay People (Apostolicam Actuositatem)*, no. 2.

57. See also *Guidelines,* no. 128-132 and CIC no. 275, 2.

identity in any way perceived as significant by the un-churched whom he meets, or by non-Catholics or non-believers? Does his activity in everyday situations contribute positively to a credible image of the Church?

The direct impact of the deacon as a minister in these circumstances must lie somewhere between unspecified good example and overly explicit authority. Poised strategically as he is, at a point where lay and clerical modes of Christian identity intersect, the deacon faces the task of creating a new type of cleric-lay relationship. The distinction of his role seems to show forth most clearly when he embodies the impulse of Christian charity in a way that encourages and affirms his brothers and sisters in their following of Jesus, the Lord who came not to be served, but to serve. The deacon's role as leader must not be in competition or conflict with that of the laity in responsible pursuit of their proper mission, but should complement and support it.

The relationship between the deacon's ministry "in the world" and his more narrowly defined ministries of charity, liturgy and the Word performed in some ecclesiastical setting has also been touched on elsewhere.[58] It is their unity in a single concept of the deacon's "service" that must receive added attention, particularly as it involves the matter of accountability—that of the deacon to the Church and that of the Church to the deacon

For the deacon's ordination to achieve its full effect as a sacramental sign, it is necessary that the Church—the body of the faithful, whether in a universal or more particular local sense—have access to his ministerial

---

58. See also *Guidelines,* no. 28-29.

witness. This access must go beyond the person or persons immediately benefiting from the deacon's individual charitable activity; it must be possible for the faithful at large to have a "window" on the integrated dimensions of the deacon's life and ministry. There must be an awareness, or at least a well-founded presumption, of the links among the deacon's high-visibility liturgical and homiletic roles, his specific activities in the ministry of love and justice and his fidelity to the ideals of *diakonia* in the environment of the world. It is the *whole* ministry of the deacon that is the sign which nourishes, instructs and challenges—i.e., *serves*— the Church. Therefore, some practical way must be found to root this integrated witness in the public consciousness if the deacon's ministry is to be fully efficacious and respectful of its complex reality on so many interrelated levels.

This is no easy task since it tends to conflict with the typical deacon's contentment with an almost anonymous kind of influence. The deacon's characteristic humility of temperament is reinforced in this matter by his common definition of service—an act done for its own sake and for the convenience or at the direction of another, with no ulterior motive other than benefit to the other, certainly with no direct expectation of self-aggrandizement. The key to sorting out this tangle of emotions and motivations is, or course, to stress that the deacon's ordination constitutes *him* a public sign— but a sign that attracts attention to itself only to deflect it onto another reality: on the love of Jesus, revealing the Eternal God through consistent compassion and care.

Because his ordination constitutes the deacon a public person in the Church,[59] there is a degree of awkwardness in trying to keep mentally separate the otherwise "private" aspects of his life. We are still only beginning to acknowledge, much less to understand, all the consequences of the deacon's position. These consequences flow from a reflection on the indivisibility of the deacon's essential identity. Yet even when these consequences provoke some unanticipated complications,[60] it is probable that such experiences will help us to grasp more completely not only the novelty of the deacon's role, but its potential for expanding our sense of the meaning of ordained ministry. If the areas of life commonly thought of as private—e.g., marriage and family, job, community life and personal freetime activities—are understood as mysterious but integral facets of the "matter" of the deacon's sacramentality, it may even happen that a major result of his service to the Church will be a renewed appreciation of the interconnectedness of the sacred and the secular in the life of the baptized believer. Thus the deacon may help to promote, not inhibit, the proper emergence of the

59. Canons 232-293 of the revised *Code of Canon Law* describe in detail the particular ways in which a cleric's life is governed by the expectations of the faithful.

60. The incidence of divorce among married permanent deacons, e.g., has caught most dioceses unprepared for dealing with the multilevel implications of the deacon's status. Slowly but steadily, policies are being developed to address such situations with both sensitivity and consistency, in the interests of the Church, of the sacraments of matrimony and holy orders, of the order of deacons and of the individuals involved. Other issues are also emerging as potential sources of complication and conflict of values.

laity in assuming their responsibility for the progress of the Church's mission.

All of this is to suggest that the practical questions of the deacon's "placement" need to be approached with circumspection. The ministry for which the deacon is accountable to the Church is far broader than the specific duties he performs in the restricted amount of time he may devote to those high-visibility activities ordinarily associated with ministry. Despite the practical benefit of detailing the deacon's ministerial responsibilities in a formal agreement, covenant or contract, it must be acknowledged that many such agreements fail to consider the broader reality of the deacon's ministry in "the world." Subtly and unintentionally, they may reinforce the concept that "ministry" is what happens in the church building, at the parish center, in the institution or apostolate. As a twenty-four-hour-a-day ordained sign, the deacon must see that such a view of his ministry, though not without a certain limited accuracy, is basically an artificial way of describing it.

Again, this is not without significant value: No one would want the concept of the deacon's ministry to be so fluid or vaporous as to dissipate in the bright light and heat of serious examination. The Church has the right of access to the sign which the deacon exists to make real in its midst: of its nature, the sign demands public expression in moments of visible, functioning service. But, as was stated before, the truth of that ritualized form of service depends on the congruence between what the deacon's visible prominence *implies* and what the community's experience of his life *confirms*. The diocesan Church must specify its expectations of how the deacon is to serve, day in and day out, as a minister with a passionate commitment to love and justice, a reverent attention to the Word of God and a prayerful sense of how the Lord is worshipped in all the ordinary events of life.

The clarity of the deacon's role in the pastoral plan of the local Church[61] is a direct reflection of the diocesan bishop's understanding of, and commitment to, the ministry of this third rank of the ordained hierarchy. Unless the bishop can articulate how centrally the deacon is associated with him and the presbyterate in the care of the local community of faith, it is difficult to expect any real and enduring accountability from the deacon and to command any profound acceptance of the deacon by priests, religious and laity.

Of course, the pastoral plan, while it must be uniquely responsive to the bishop's concerns and direction, cannot be totally determined by his imagination and honor his priorities and expectations alone. Beyond even the mandated consultative processes of listening which he must observe, there are some inherent properties in the ecclesial reality that the bishop, too, must respect in his exercise of faithful stewardship. Surely among these are the basic identities of the ordained ministries. It is unrealistic, and perhaps wrong, to suppose that the character of the diaconate, even in just its diocesan embodiment, can be fundamentally reshaped to fit the particular programs and priorities of successive bishops. A bishop will do well if he simply invites the diocesan diaconate, by example as much as by direction, to faithful adherence to common ideals of diaconal

61. *Guidelines,* no. 49-51.

servanthood centering on his dependence upon his deacons for collaboration in the mission for which he is uniquely accountable. It will be valuable if he can enunciate, with sensitivity to a core diaconal identity, how he sees the deacon's function as having a pastoral focus in relation to the diocesan Church's witness to charity.

This crucial relationship of understanding and acceptance by the bishop is not, by all accounts, as positive or comprehensive as many deacons—and many bishops—would wish. The overwhelmingly affirming, if occasionally vague, expression of support by the majority of U.S. bishops on numerous public occasions[62] are, not infrequently, followed in everyday speech and action by more noncommittal or perplexed assurances. It is healthy that the 1984 U.S. bishops' guidelines put strong emphasis on the indispensable importance of articulating, clearly and convincingly, the *need* for diaconal ministry in light of the diocesan pastoral plan.[63] The basic question is simple: How does the order of deacons help us to be Church? With the answer to that question sketched out in at least its general perspectives, guidelines can be developed that would govern the ministerial expectations of the individual deacon.

The general perspectives of the diocesan pastoral plan should recognize the deacon's strategic natural place-

---

62. For example, the vote on the revised U.S. *Guidelines* in 1984 found only five bishops opposed to the text; yet several dozen dioceses have not implemented the restoration of the permanent diaconate. And the comments of Archbishop Pilarczyk and Cardinal Bernardin at the 1986 gathering of bishops at Collegeville, Minnesota (cited above, footnote 1) clearly reveal a degree of ambivalence that suggests the need for continuing study and familiarization.

63. *Guidelines,* no. 49.

ment, as well as indicate his role in the specific ritualized services discussed above. It should be plain to the deacon that the Church looks to him for expressions of his sign of service "in the world"—within the environments of home and family, of neighborhood and community, of job, recreation and cultural life—for creative and compelling expressions that will nourish and affirm the impulse to charity and service sown in the believer at baptism.

In particular, the pastoral plan should avoid descriptions of the deacon's role that tie him too closely to custodial pastoral responsibilities. This requires great care because the forces are strong that would identify the deacon primarily as one ordained to be a stand-in for the presbyter or as an available approximation of a priest, a substitute useful in extreme situations but who is then distinguished mainly by what he *cannot* do (Mass, Confession, etc.) or by his status as a married man (with marriage seen almost as the factor that disqualifies him from a more truly vital service). Among these forces is the shortage of priests in some dioceses for duty as resident pastors. While the 1984 guidelines acknowledge the possibility of deacons emerging to serve as community leaders with some quasi-presbyteral responsibilities, it can be noted that there is a subtle ambivalence evident in the way the guidelines address the subject.[64] It is an ambivalence that surfaces from time to time as the Church tries to integrate its sense of a properly diaconal role with its dominant experience of the presbyteral model of ministerial leadership. It suffices to suggest that a diocesan Church,

---

64. Ibid., no. 44-45.

when confronted with a lack of sufficient priest personnel, should perhaps first exhaust the other possible alternatives allowed by Canon Law,[65] before resorting to the deacon as the stand-in of choice, solely on the basis of his ordination. The risk is that the diaconate, still in its infancy, is more vulnerable to having its identity as a distinctive ordained ministry gobbled up by the presbyteral expectations of a congregation. The deacon will certainly be an important figure in the equation that tries to resolve the problems raised by the growing shortage of priests—but he should be permitted to make a contribution that respects the distinctiveness of his order rather than presumes on its relative adequacy as "next best" in the line of ordained ministries. Such an attitude really does not secure recognition or acceptance for diaconate as essential in itself; nor do the various efforts, by deacons and others, to promote a more "clerical" identity for the deacon by employing the forms and symbols commonly associated with the presbyteral order.[66]

The opposite tendency should also be noted, i.e., the

---

65. CIC no. 517, 2.

66. Cf. *Guidelines*, no.130. The 1984 revision shifts the emphasis from a presumption that clerical garb will usually *not* be worn, to a recognition that a diocesan bishop may authorize the customary wearing of some distinctive attire. It is not necessary to read 'distincitive' as meaning the traditional Roman collar, etc., and the paragraph does refer to the "exceptional circumstances" that may lead a bishop to determine a policy qualifying the exemption granted by the *Code of Canon Law* (no. 288). During the floor discussion before the bishops' conference voted on the revised *Guidelines*, the question of whether a bishop could still *prohibit* the wearing of traditional clerical attire was answered by the chair in the affirmative.

attitude that thoroughly discounts the deacon's identity as in any real way making a distinctive contribution to the Church. For all the declarations about the diaconate as an essential ministry, it is curious that whole nations and regions, like some dioceses even in the U.S., have determined that they can get along without it within the boundaries of their jurisdiction. In its most disturbing form, this attitude is revealed in the studied ignoring of a deacon's ordained status in some dioceses that have not introduced the restored diaconate. To the extent that the disinterest or opposition of bishops, priests and others forces a careful reformulation of our understandings about this order, it is a salutary influence. But it surely must yield at some point to a tolerant acceptance of the deacon's identity, even if it is not precipitately embraced.

Despite legitimate concerns about the restored diaconate's influence (Is its exclusively male character under present legislation an unacceptable example of sexism? Is its clerical status another way of postponing acceptance of genuine lay leadership?), there are other methods of addressing them than resisting the order itself or ignoring it entirely. Our whole experience with the restoration needs to be continually evaluated. Problems need to be admitted and corrected; reform and renewal need to be pursued, respectful of the rights and dignity of all persons in the Church. But it is perilous for us to accept a principle of selectivity that allows a local Church unilaterally to determine that the validity of an ordained ministry is in practice not recognized in its territory.[67]

---

67. For example, canon 764 properly qualifies the dea-

Principles of Deacon Placement

The dioceses that have implemented the restoration bear the responsibility for demonstrating to skeptics how, in fact, this new/old ministry strengthens the local Church. Their convictions in this regard will be reflected in their principles of placement and accountability. Deacons, too, share this responsibility; by concentrating on the distinctive qualities of their ministerial identity, deacons will contribute best to this effort to enrich the entire Church by restoring this order to its proper place.

The first principle of placement centers on the deacon's responsibility for an essential dimension of local Christian life, namely the vitality of its witness of charity. If the Church is not truly the Church unless it is active in imitation of Christ's charity,[68] then it would seem the deacon's service must be linked preeminently to this aspect of the Church's fidelity. Through the permanence and public character of his commitment in ordination, the deacon is entrusted with a responsibility not just to be faithful in charity himself, but to see that the Church remains faithful as well. It pertains to the deacon, under the authority of the bishop and in association with presbyters, to fan into steady flame the spark of Christian charity that should characterize

con's universal faculty for preaching, but the mere mention of that faculty should underscore the significance of the deacon's ministry and the respect it should command as a matter of course.

68. *Lumen Gentium*, no. 42 provides a moving meditation about charity as the perfection of Christian holiness.

a believing community. That will require a sensitivity both to the needs of the local and larger communities and to the potential for response in the hearts and resources of the Church. Such sensitivity should be presumed always to be functioning, able to register the subtle changes in the climate of need and charitable response and ready to affect that climate in a positive way, both through direct personal action and through challenge and encouragement of others.

It is important for the bishop, at the center of the circles of ordained ministers in a diocese, to appreciate what it means for the Church to have such a presence placed "in the world." The consistency of the deacon's faithfulness to his responsibility in that multidimensional environment may be considered by the bishop as the necessary prerequisite to the deacon's exercise of his more ritualized functions.[69] It is the bishop who can best articulate what the deacon's "faculties" presuppose; indeed, only the bishop can authoritatively call the deacon to accountability for the impact made by his ministry "in the world." Yet, although most deacons are probably aware that their presence is perceived to make a difference in the everyday circumstances of family, neighborhood and workplace, fewer would consider that their effectiveness in those spheres is a ministerial expectation their bishop has of them. Whatever mechanism of accountability is adopted in a given diocese, it should perhaps start with a clear expression of the bishop's sense that the deacon serves the mission of the diocesan Church—and extends the

---

69. *Guidelines*, no. 49-50, 128-129, 132.

bishop's own pastoral care for that entire Church—in the areas that provide a real test of the Church's identity as a witness to the saving action of Christ.

Secondly, with expectations set for the deacon's ministry "in the world," the other aspects of his placement can be considered. Since he receives canonical faculties for the administration of sacraments and the exercise of a preaching office, the deacon must recognize his duty to permit the believing community a full and rounded access to his witness, as was discussed above. The point in ordaining a deacon is to establish him as that ritual sign, an official minister who can act and speak with an authority related to the responsibility entrusted to him. He is ordained not for his own sake, but for the good of the Church. Unless impeded by a serious reason,[70] the deacon must expect to devote time and energy to the threefold ministries of charity, liturgy and the Word that are the ritual celebration of his daily ministry "in the world." Through such activities, the deacon speaks to the collective consciousness of the believing community, focusing its attention on fidelity to the call to follow the Servant Christ.

---

70. It is possible to apply the broadest possible interpretation to the various kinds of activities that express each of the three focuses of diaconal ministry. However, there may still be occasions or circumstances when a deacon must curtail his activity in one or another area and yet remain a deacon in good standing: e.g., age, health, particular problems in a given area of ministry. These considerations and others may render it advisable for a deacon to relinquish certain duties. The principle, however, should be that an integrated, threefold ministry is the expected norm. Of course, it is not the deacon's right simply too withdraw unilaterally from an area of ministry.

Thirdly, it is appropriate to set limits—both a minimum and a maximum—to the amount of time given to these ritualized activities, principally to maintain balance in the perception of what the deacon is for. It is too easy, as has been mentioned, for the deacon—who is typically a person with a great desire *not* to say no in any circumstance in which he might be of help—to be swept up in the myriad liturgical and teaching tasks that are so prominent and visible in the local Catholic congregation. But, even though giving assistance in such tasks is certainly a way in which the deacon definitely "serves" the community (simultaneously providing the necessary access to his sacramental identity), it is not the chief reason why deacons are ordained. A minimum expectation is desirable, to assure the local community its ritual access to the deacon's sacramentality; and a maximum limit is also desirable, to preserve the distinctiveness, first of the deacon's focus on the virtue of charity and then, of his primary placement "in the world." The limits that are detailed in each case will most likely have to be interpreted with some flexibility due precisely to the deacon's immersion in responsibilities that will often impose unexpected demands on his availability. Tensions can be minimized by carefully evaluating the program responsibilities that may be assigned the deacon and by the deacon's recognition of the importance of some reliable structure in his ministry, to let his witness speak more clearly to the community.

Fourth, whatever figure is determined as the target minimum/maximum average, it seems helpful to suggest strongly that, within that average figure, a clear majority of the time and activity should be associated with the ministry of charity, since that remains the distinctive feature of the deacon's identity. Certainly the focus on recognizably charitable activities must never be entirely lost or even substantially obscured by the prominence of a deacon's ministries of liturgy and the Word. Indeed, should any abridgment of his duties be necessary, it is the deacon's charitable ministry that should be reduced last. The fact that one is ordained to be a sign of service with a particular accent on charity should give those aspects of a deacon's ministry a practical priority in his and the diocese's expectations.

Fifth, one area of the deacon's natural placement is the parish in which he resides. Often, it becomes the locus of the deacon's formal assignment by the bishop. There is an obvious value to this practice, since it builds on the strength of the mutual familiarity between the deacon and the particular community. However, there are also rather obvious potential difficulties inherent in such an arrangement. One might hope that, with good will and sincere effort and with a deacon who really demonstrates the kind of personal flexibility that appears to be characteristic of an effective deacon, the difficulties can be successfully managed for the good of the Church. Also important in this regard is the clarity of the bishop's expectations of the deacon's ministry in the given parish. It must be acknowledged by all, though not as an occasion for arrogance by the deacon, that he is assigned by the bishop, not engaged by the pastor or congregation, to have a particular effect on the life of the parish related to its own diaconal character. Coordination of this ministry and accountability for it will be exercised by and through the pastor, without prejudice to his authority under the bishop.

Yet it must also be clear that theologically the deacon is related directly to the bishop and that his ministry, like that of the presbyter, is a diocesan responsibility, not limited to the confines of a particular parish or other pastoral unit. In fact, it may be said that a deacon is "placed" in a parish precisely to unite it with the diocesan bishop in solidarity in the matter of Christian charity.

Lest it seem that difficulties in a deacon's assignment to his home parish (or any other parish, for that matter) are related solely to the pastor or to other priests and staff-persons, it must be admitted that a deacon's familiarity with the community itself can sometimes make him vulnerable to manipulation by his neighbors and fellow parishioners. This may result from a misunderstanding about his role and responsibility and may reflect simply the people's overexposure to the presbyteral model of ordained ministry. Again, clarity in the deacon's own mind is essential, as is a proper catechesis about his identity and enforcement by the diocese of certain standards governing the deacon's involvement in parish life. Those standards should recognize the value to the diocese of having a diaconal minister with intimate appreciation of a community, its needs and its potential. The deacon's home parish, even if it does not figure in his official assignment, is nonetheless an integral part of his natural placement. It is better for the diocese and the parish to build on that factor rather than to resist or ignore it.

But, as has just been suggested, the diocesan bishop must be sensitive, too, to the need in all parish communities for the sign of *diakonia* to be lived in its expression as an ordained ministry. While there is much to be said for promoting the ministry of the deacon by seeking candidates in each parish, the bishop may choose to place deacons in parishes other than that in which they reside because of special needs in the parish or because of special qualities in the deacon. It is important, of course, that such assignments not be artificial, but respectful of the necessity for a deacon's *entire* ministry to be somehow beneficial for the community, not just the high profile functions associated with liturgy and the Word. A deacon should have the opportunity to establish a degree or relatedness with a community, sufficient to assure a mutual familiarity that will be the primary vehicle for the accomplishment of his diaconal mission. He serves that mission by witnessing to the centrality of charity as the earthly Body of Christ pursues its task of proclaiming with authority the kingdom of God.

The deacon, too, must be careful to insure that his own concept of his placement flows from conviction about the nature of his distinctive role. Since his actual schedule of ritualized activities will often be determined, or at least heavily influenced, by needs enunciated by others, he will have to balance his natural desire to be helpful with a skillful assertion of his distinctive emphasis on functions of charitable service. The sense in which a deacon is considered to be a rather generalized "helper," available for whatever needs doing—a realistic element in his self-understanding, to be sure—must be broadened and deepened to recognize the particular character of his sacramental witness in searching out the truly needy and responding to their plight. Granted the typical deacon's readiness to lend a hand in almost any enterprise that will assist another, it will demand an especially thoughtful assessment of how his cooperation in a number of conventional activities will either contribute to that witness or obscure the radical link between the deacon and outreach to the contemporary *anawim*.[71] Among these activities, it would seem, are common administrative, managerial and custodial tasks directly related to the Church, routine catechetical duties, heavy liturgical and sacramental schedules, etc. Some regular presence in each of these is understandable and probably advisable from the point of view of publicizing the deacon's responsibility. But prudence should dictate caution in allowing the deacon's time to be unevenly distributed in such tasks.

It seems reasonable, as was suggested elsewhere, that the deacon's ministries of liturgy and the Word should reflect his preoccupation with the ministry of love and justice.[72] So, for example, his service as a liturgical minister might focus particularly on aiding those whose access to the community's worship is restricted: the deacon, e.g., might not only bring sacramental service to those in such need (the homebound, the disabled, etc.) but might coordinate other services to them and promote other ways of the community's including them. And his familiarity with their situation should find an outlet in his speaking up on their behalf before others who can meet some of their physical, emotional and social needs. Or, in another example, the deacon's role as a proclaimer of the Word and homilist might serve

---

71. In a conscientious, mission-oriented Church, at least the deacon surely should be sensitive to the presence and needs of the poorest of the poor.

72. *Guidelines,* no. 43.

as the opportunity for the voiceless to find their voice and for the community to examine its conscience in matters of charity and justice, in everyday situations and in a more global context. What ought to be applauded in a deacon's homily is not just the correctness of his theology and his lucidity of expression, but above all the clarity of his moral vision in encouraging his listeners to a more integral practice of Christian love. His role in the community's catechumenal and baptismal ministry might utilize the deacon less as organizer and instructor, and more as welcomer and facilitator. His participation in sacramental preparation might serve to highlight the obligation of charity as a believer moves through the stages of initiation. As a kind of coach or mentor, for example, deacons have certainly proved themselves helpful to young people approaching confirmation. And often with their wives, deacons have been moderators and promoters of service to couples contemplating marriage, as well as to those struggling faithfully in the reality of married life. Perhaps the deacon's focus, in dealing with married couples or those preparing for marriage, could take its cue from the blessing in the rite of marriage that calls on God to sustain the couple so that "the needy may find in you generous friends."[73]

In administration, for example, the deacon should probably be used less as a secularly proficient manager and more as one who looks to building up the community's resources for service to those in need. His participation in consultative bodies like the parish council, for example, might better be tied to his ability

---

73. *Rite of Marriage*, no. 125.

to represent those who are otherwise unseen and unheard and to tend the flame of charity in the hearts of the group.

Whatever their form, then, the precise expectations of the deacon's activity, it would seem, should bear the unmistakable accent of his fundamental orientation as a sign of Christ's love for the least of his brothers and sisters.[74]

---

74. Cf. Matthew 25:31-46.

Process of Placement and Accountability

When the focus of the deacon's distinctive role is clear, then the process of detailing his particular responsibilities can find its proper context. The covenant or ministry agreement or contract which many dioceses already use, is a helpful way for the diocese to assure that the placement of a deacon responds to genuine needs and safeguards the fundamental character of the diaconate. It is also a fruitful first step toward a process of evaluation that will be productive for the deacon's growth as a minister.

Experience has demonstrated the value of considerable specificity in any such agreement, in detailing both the expectations of all parties and the anticipated schedule and timelines to be observed. Where such specificity is neglected, through confusion over the deacon's role, or excessive casualness or overdone regard for "spontaneity," the effort usually succeeds only in setting the deacon up for eventual conflict and discouragement. Even with the specific detailing of expectations and mutual responsibilities, of course, there should be enough flexibility to permit necessary and sensible adjustments. Perhaps the one nonnegotiable element in any agreement, and the one provision to be rigidly adhered to, should be regular, mutual, face-to-face communication between the deacon and his immediate supervisor. Both the duties and the qualifications of supervisors need to be carefully spelled out and accepted, but in such a way that the more or less unique character of a deacon's identity in ministry is properly respected.

The agreement should reflect the daily context of the deacon's ministry "in the world," stating general expectations perhaps established by the diocesan bishop. The interplay between this larger context of ministry and the more limited segment spent in the public, ritualized expressions of ministry, whether in parishes, institutions, diocesan apostolates, etc., should be fully appreciated by all parties. The deacon must be ready to rein in his natural bent toward acquiescing to almost any request and accept only those ritual responsibilities that he can reasonably expect to fulfill. Where the deacon finds the circumstances of his life too unsettled to permit an adequate routine of such high-profile ritual activity, he should perhaps consider a temporary withdrawal from "active status," since his presence and performance are integral elements in his being experienced by the Church as a sacrament of the Servant Christ.

The relative artificiality of this recourse is readily admitted, since the Church can typically count on the deacon's use of his talents for helpful service even when he is not officially "on duty." But it is offered as a way of reconciling the occasional unpredictability of the deacon's circumstances with the Church's right to an integral ministry expressed fully in recognizable activities of love and justice, liturgy and the Word. The rhythms of a typical deacon's life may even require periodic resort to such temporary status and this must not be interpreted as delinquence, but as respect for the complex role-definition of this order in its contemporary expression. To be sure, a deacon who seeks to be relieved for a time of certain commitments so that he can honor other, preexisting obligations (family, job, etc.) more single-mindedly, is still exerting a powerful influence for good in the Church. Such conscientiousness, though it usually induces regret in the deacon himself, should probably be regarded as nothing other than a phase of his multidimensional ministry.

An agreement that specifies the various expectations of a deacon's ministry—his own, those of the diocesan Church, those of the particular placement—is a primary tool for accountability and evaluation. Again, experience demonstrates that deacons, most likely because of their highly sensitive relational instinct, derive benefit more from a personal discussion of their activity than from less participatory procedures. In such conversations, it would be important to include the larger context of the deacon's placement, that beyond his "assignment" to ministry in a parish, institution, apostolate, etc. A supervisor or mentor may help the deacon more by giving him a chance to talk about his service "in the world" than by immediately focusing on even the positive points noticed in his more limited, formal duties performed in and through "Church" activities. The deacon is more easily affirmed thereby in his basic community-building and nurturing talent, which is of greater practical significance both for him and for the Church. Other, more ritualized functions are certainly important and need to be supported and critiqued. But the lasting, truly diaconal impact of those activities will depend enormously on the depth and health of their roots in his witness to charity in the environments that occupy so much of his daily attention.

Diocesan evaluations, too, need to devote more effort to calling forth an accountability for this "ordinary" diaconal ministry—or at least as much effort as is commonly directed to the more "extraordinary" activities that serve to celebrate and ritualize the diaconal identity. The diocese can accomplish this in a variety of ways. Regular, personal meetings with the deacon by the bishop or, more likely, by a diocesan vicar for deacons and program director, are valuable, but deacon-to-deacon contact can be even more productive. A deacon responds enthusiastically to the affirmation that springs from an encounter with a kindred spirit, one who understands the impulses that drive a deacon and who shares the same experience. This kind of support is different even from that of the wife of the married deacon who is most often an expert in communicating appreciation for the inner dynamics that fuel the deacon's sense of service and his commitment to it. A brother deacon understands from a similar experience what it is like to be immersed "in the world" and at home in it, and yet in a radical way not "of it," the bearer of a responsibility that enhances and energizes one's relationship with it but which also detaches one from it, as the embodiment of a challenge that seeks the most authentic realization of its potential. His is a passionate concern for the Church, his fellow believers, in dialogue with that "world"—and so the deacon is more acutely sensitive to the ways in which the encounter can be discouraging and bruising, or distracting and tempting. He is somewhat removed from some of the dynamics of that world—its competitiveness, self-centeredness and superficiality—usually by temperament and as reinforced by ordination and an awareness of the Church's expectations. Someone else who shares the curious complexity of that relationship can contribute both to easing some of the frustration and to rekindling the sense of purpose that impels one to be a servant for others.

Retreats, support groups, recollection experiences can all be used to reaffirm the deacon's identity as servant. Continuing education programs, too, should aim at more than the imparting of information or skill for more proficient functioning. Better, they should acknowledge simultaneously the deacon's need for affirmation and refinement of those talents that mark him as one to whom others will turn instinctively for understanding and help. Such a man's diaconal character is advertised more by his active service of love and justice than by any title or publicized job description. When his diaconal core is thus strengthened, there should be added motivation for the deacon to develop further the specific skills that will make of his "extraordinary ministry" a more self-conscious and effective sacramental medium. In particular, the deacon will be appreciated for the perceptive heart that allows him to see the images and hear the voices of human need, and for the selflessness that frees him to respond with his time, energy and personal resources. In such a deacon indeed, the Church should see reflected something essential about itself and an incarnational expression of its Servant Lord.

In Closing

Twenty-one years after Paul VI published norms inviting the world's Catholic bishops to restore the diaconate as a permanent order, as the Second Vatican Council had called for,[75] there is a record to be reviewed, there are lessons to be drawn, from the experience in the United States. The Church in the United States has implemented the restoration of the diaconate with greater enthusiasm than any other national community of Catholics. This imposes on us a responsibility for examining the record—not just once, but repeatedly, as we live longer with and gain greater familiarity with this order of ministry. To fail to do so would be to neglect a duty we owe the universal Church, to share the results of our efforts to respond to God's gifts, and it would betray the generous dedication of those who have personally borne the burden of reintroducing the Church to the deacon as one ordained to a permanent ministry.

This ongoing examination, however, is not simply a matter of comparing what has emerged in the actual diaconate with a detailed original blueprint. It is clear that the foundational documents of the restoration were

---

75. *Lumen Gentium*, no. 29.

117

short on specifics and were content to sketch some broad outlines to guide the early experience.[76] Into the gaps flowed a variety of wide-ranging expectations, not all of them easily reconciled with each other, and some of them unreasonable. Still, they all have had a part to play in arousing our critical senses, so that our review of the experience is never really neutral. Perhaps no other area of the deacon's identity is more likely to reveal the clash between expectations and results than the "ministry of service." We have seen how this phrase has an inherent ambiguity,[77] and have opted to use it as a description of the entire context of the deacon's role rather than as a distinct component of it.

Treating the deacon's "ministry of service" as the context within which he exercises ministries of charity, liturgy and the Word, one is then in a stronger position to test the essentially responsive character of the deacon's role: How, in fact, do his ministries of charity, liturgy and the Word "serve" the Church? How must they be shaped and positioned so as to exert a truly sacramental influence in the Church, which is itself called to respond to a series of specific demands for signs of fidelity? To say that the deacon serves by way of good example, though true enough in its limited sense,[78] is an inadequate explanation of the distinction wrought by the sacrament of holy orders in which the deacon participates.[79]

Part of the difficulty may stem from our habit of so individualizing our concept of sacramental ordination

---

76. *Guidelines,* Preface, p. 2.
77. Cf. ibid., Introduction, p. 9.
78. Ibid., pp. 24ff.
79. *Lumen Gentium,* no. 29.

that we risk losing an understanding of its radically corporate significance. It is important to reflect that the whole body of believers "receives" the sacrament of orders, in and through the ordination and service of some of its members as bishops, presbyters and deacons. Indeed, the point of such ordination is to assure the community of continued access to a service that will strengthen its life, through functions of ritual celebration, authentic teaching and governance, in the name of Jesus and according to his Gospel.[80] Unless ordination is restricted simply to its sense as a juridical act with a profound effect on the person of the ordained, principally at the ritual high-point of the laying-on of hands, it is clear that the entire community is intended to be the beneficiary of that person's designation for the rest of his life. His relationship to the family of believers is forever altered. Bound together in a lasting embrace of great spiritual power, the ordained and the Church experience a mutuality of call and mission that extends the sacramental reality of holy orders. The effectiveness of this mystery is not limited to moments of authoritative ritual activity. Rather, the life of the ordained in its entirety is "at the service" of the community, directed toward its nourishment and guidance, its affirmation and healing. It is a word spoken in a dialogue whose effectiveness is judged by the vitality of Christian witness in that corner of the world and those settings of human endeavor where the believers gather and live out their faith.

This "receptivity" on the part of the believing community is not envisioned as passivity or as providing

---

80. Ibid., no. 11.

the background against which the ordained operate. The community has a life with a distinctive dynamism, but it is always essentially expressed in its communion with Jesus. The servanthood of the ordained is a means of facilitating this communion, which has its intended result in the Church's fidelity, in all its members, to his Gospel. This servanthood, in turn, is expressed in manifold ways. In the case of the deacon, the ministries of charity, liturgy and the Word structure his relationship to the community as a sign in which all find their Christian identity brought to clearer focus, wherein it can be challenged and affirmed. The deacon, in all he does, is to contribute to the authenticity of this expression; the message for which he supplies the visible and audible "word"—in clear and contemporary accents—is Christ's: " ' . . . as I have done for you, you should also do. . . . ' "[81] The inner consistency of his life with this command of the Lord will prove far more powerful a means of communication than his execution, however expert, of ministerial tasks, and will constitute the real substance of his ministry of service. That expertise must not be neglected. Being an effective sign requires more than casual good intentions. But at its heart must lie a conviction that the deacon is preeminently an instrument of Christ's servanthood.

Like the boy in the gospel account who could offer only five loaves and two fishes to feed the multitude,[82] the deacon must not be overwhelmed by the seeming poverty of even his strongest gifts and talents, but should present them generously to Christ and see them mar-

---

81. John 13:12-15.
82. Cf. John 6:9.

velously transformed for the nourishment of his people. He does this by entering into a relationship with the Church for life and with the totality of his life: by representing as genuinely as he can—in the depths of his sensitivity to human needs for sympathetic attention, in the vigor of his compassionate assistance—the Christ who leads by serving.

It is the image of that Christ which the restoration of the permanent diaconate has proposed to revitalize with a more fully conscious sacramental sign. It seeks to find the auras of that image in the hearts and lives of believers and confirm them. It seeks to carry that image into all manner of action in the world, to refresh those whose spirits resonate to the message of Jesus and to strengthen the Church's collective witness to its Lord. The deacon's ministry of service addresses us all and calls us to faithful, creative participation in the servanthood of Jesus Christ. May it grow well as this special sign, nurtured in turn by the fidelity of all believers to the challenge of following a Servant Lord.

About the Author

Rev. Timothy J. Shugrue is a priest of the Archdiocese of Newark, New Jersey. A native of Elizabeth, New Jersey, he was educated at Seton Hall University and Immaculate Conception Seminary, where he received his Master's degree in theology. Father Shugrue served in parish ministry in Jersey City and was chaplain at an archdiocesan high school before becoming director of the Permanent Diaconate Preparation Program in 1979. In 1982 he became director of the Office of the Permanent Diaconate, responsible for both the formation and post-ordination programs.

Father Shugrue has served as president of the National Association of Permanent Diaconate Directors, in which capacity he participated as a consultant for the Bishops' Committee on the Permanent Diaconate. He has also been a participant in ecumenical discussions sponsored by the National Council of Churches investigating experiences and theories of diaconal ministry in the various Christian churches. Father Shugrue was the 1987 recipient of the William L. Philbin Award of the National Association of Permanent Diaconate Directors.